100
Inspiring STORIES

Finding
Love and Laughter
Hope and Healing
Forgiveness and Faith

Teresa Pirola

XXIII

TWENTY-THIRD PUBLICATIONS
Mystic, CT 06355

Twenty-Third Publications
185 Willow Street
P.O. Box 180
Mystic, CT 06355
(860) 536-2611
(800) 321-0411

First published in 1998 by E.J. Dwyer (Australia) Pty Ltd.

ISBN: 0-89622-942-4
Library of Congress Catalog Card Number: 98-61013
Printed in the U.S.A.

Dedication

To Peter and Chele,
a love story that had to be told

With many such parables
he spoke the word to them.

— Mark 4:33

Table of Contents

Introduction 1

1. Stories of hope 3

2. Stories of grieving and healing 13

3. Stories of forgiveness.....................23

4. Stories of faith...............................33

5. Stories about tough decisions 43

6. Stories of prayer 53

7. Stories of simplicity.........................63

8. Stories of community 73

9. Stories of justice 83

10. Stories about not giving up 93

11. Stories of witness 103

12. Stories of joy...............................113

Index of Gospel readings....................126

100 Inspiring Stories

Introduction

I started "collecting" stories about ten years ago. Not so much stories from books and magazines; rather, I wrote down the "quiet" variety, the anecdotes and insights observed and spoken in the events and conversations that filled my life and the lives of those around me.

My reason for doing so was something of a personal nature. My life, at the time, was rough sailing: a broken romance, an overwhelming sense of loss, untold grief.

Paradoxically, the same period was one of enormous external productivity. While I was receiving accolades for my achievements in church work, I was acutely aware that privately I was facing the greatest gospel challenge of my life—whether to give up or keep going, to believe or turn my back on God, to love the church or hate it.

The irony of the situation was all too apparent to me. My external achievements were praised while my inner battle, a struggle of far greater proportions and significance, went hidden and unacknowledged. I began to ask myself questions: what was the gospel really about? Could it be that the church which preaches the centrality of Christ's death and resurrection was more interested in my latest lenten program than in whether or not I was "rising from the dead"? A life lesson was becoming painfully clear: there are no awards given for simply getting out of bed in the morning when feel like you would rather be dead.

Through this experience I became more attuned to the presence of bereaved people in our midst. I wondered why their grief made us so uncomfortable. While the church community tried to care for them (that is, to make them "better"), I could not see that we really tried to learn from them. Here we had people intensely engaged in the death-resurrection process so central to the Christian mystery. Why didn't anyone seek out their wisdom or their insights?

I deeply wanted to make the wisdom and insights of these people available to the wider community. So I began to collect stories from everyday life—not just about bereavement but about all kinds of gospel wisdom.

Stories from real people in real life invite readers to see the holiness within themselves. The act of storytelling implicitly says: your own story is praiseworthy, your life reflections sacred. These moments of insight, often arising from simple and mundane events, are given to ordinary people as prophetic gifts. They illuminate a deeper wisdom, the footprints of grace in our lives.

How easily the significance of these moments can escape our notice! Hoodwinked by society's norms, we can think that important things are said only by academics and celebrities, that important events are only those which make the headlines on the six o'clock news. Yet it is precisely in the gift of ordinary moments that we most learn from and teach one another. Indeed, it was through parables about ordinary moments and through the sharing of life stories that Jesus taught the gospel.

Each day is an opportunity to grow, to learn, and to enter more deeply into the mystery of God's love simply by living with an awareness of God's grace at work in the present moment.

1

*Stories
of Hope*

Someone else's garbage

A religious sister working in the Philippines writes: I'm slowly settling into Smokey Mountain (Smokey Mountain is actually a giant garbage heap in Manila, the Philippines, where many of the city's poor live). It is a sad, sad place. I get most upset about the children living in such squalor and filth. Yesterday I saw a group of them playing with a huge, dead rat.

There is also another side to life here. Like the day I was walking around Smokey with a guide and I said, "I'll never find my way around here." She was quite surprised by my comment and said, "Look for the decorations." I wanted to say "I don't see decorations, I only see trash!" but I held my tongue and decided to pray for a change of vision.

It seems a miracle to me, but I am now beginning to see decorations and not just garbage. I still sit in disbelief that these people can have so much hope and faith, when all they have is what seems to be someone else's trash. (Kerry; courtesy *Caritas Australia*)

Ripple effect

A young man turned up at the local parish inquiring as to how he could become a Christian. A parishioner welcomed him and began to ask him a bit about himself.

"Last year I was in jail," said the young man. "During the time I served, some guys in jail got involved in a program which explained what Christianity was about. I did not get involved, but I saw such a change in them that I thought: 'When I get out of this place I'm going to investigate what the church has to offer.'" (AN)

Your story _____

- *Think of a time when you chose hope over despair. What thoughts and feelings have, at times, threatened your sense of hope?*
- *What keeps your sense of hope alive and growing through dark times?*

4

Doing time

Life in jail is tough. The accommodations are spartan, the food is ordinary, and the sense of someone else running your life is debilitating. The men are locked in their cells from 4:30 PM to 9.00 AM, usually with another inmate (whose company is not of their choosing). Because of the drug abuse that goes on, people's reactions can be unpredictable and violent. It is not a safe environment. Paranoia is rife. They say you do not have a friend in jail.

It was into a situation such as this that a small team of Christians ventured to run a three-day program, giving inmates an opportunity to talk about life in a Christian context. We spent some months preparing for the program, which included follow-up sessions for the twenty participating inmates.

I had never been involved with anything like prison ministry before and the experience turned out to be mindblowing for prisoners and presenters alike. It is incredible to realize that God's love is powerful enough to touch the most hardened places of our hearts. To be present as these men opened up and shared their loneliness, their burdens, and their new found hope was indeed a humbling privilege. (Tony)

Woman of hope

The most profound statement of Easter faith I have ever heard was the comment of a woman facing the untimely death of her husband. Seeing the fear etched in the faces of her married friends and relatives as they contemplated the possibility of such tragedy happening to them, she said: "I represent every couple's greatest fear…and I am also their greatest hope." (Anna)

Your story _____

- *Describe the "darkest" situation you have ever faced. What ray of light managed to pierce that darkness?*
- *How and when have you been a ray of light in another's darkness?*

Wrap with love

"We should not be overwhelmed by the enormity of suffering. We fear we can only do a little... but all the little efforts have made our success story."(Sonia Gidley-King)

When we hear United Nations estimates that ten to twenty million bone-cold people in the world may die tonight, most of us cluck our tongues and change the TV channel. Sonia Gidley-King, however, a widow who had recently faced her second bout of major surgery, asked herself what she could do to help. Compelled out of her armchair and into her closets in search of leftover yarn, Sonia's desire to knit a blanket or warm wrap was already expanding into a bigger idea.

The result? Wrap with Love, a project of "humans caring about other humans." By mobilizing people all over the country to knit, crochet, or weave a blanket (or donate their leftover yarn), Sonia devised a practical and communal way to express concern for people in war zones and natural disaster areas who are suffering from the effects of cold weather. Between 1992 and 1996, approximately 17,000 blankets and wraps were shipped to countries like Rwanda, Romania, the Ukraine, and Croatia. The blankets are also donated to the homeless and needy in this country, as well.

Wrap with Love is not a registered charity. Supported by major aid agencies, all help is voluntary. Said one contributor, "It gives you an inner satisfaction somehow to know that you are doing something for somebody else. I know I am only a small cog in a vast wheel but without those little cogs the wheel doesn't turn."

Your story _____

- *Who are some people who could be described as "prophets of hope" in your neighborhood? in your country? in the wider world?*
- *What qualities do you think contribute to the making of a hope-filled person?*

4) MATTHEW 9:9–13
Those who are well have no need of a physician, but those who are sick

Maggie

"Don't expect anything from Maggie," said the nursing home attendant. "She never opens her eyes. She sits huddled all day, almost comatose. There is really not much you can do for her except to massage her hands a bit." I was an occupational therapy student being briefed on the morning of my one-day practicum. My task was to involve the residents in a range of stimulating activities. They were lovely people and generally quite responsive to me. But not Maggie. As predicted, she sat like a stone statue, apparently seeing nothing, hearing nothing, and responding to no one.

I went up close to her ear and said, "I know there is a beautiful person in there," and continued to talk softly to her. As the day progressed, I sang to her and read some poetry. I had been told she never went outside, so I went out and gathered rose petals, pressed them into her hands and held them up to her nose. By the end of the day, as I told her I had to go, she looked no different. Maggie was still Maggie.

As I headed for the door, I realized I had left the poetry book behind and turned to retrieve it. To my utter amazement there was Maggie, sitting upright, head lifted, eyes wide open. Brilliant, clear blue eyes. Recovering from my shock I went back to her, talking and interacting with her with renewed vigor. As I left the nursing home later, I spoke to the nursing attendant and pressed her for more details about Maggie's condition. The woman was adamant. "There's really nothing to say. We never get a peep out of Maggie. And she never opens her eyes."

Not long after that day Maggie died. I never had the chance to really understand what was going on inside her frail body. But I will never forget her eyes. There was life in those eyes...beautiful, clear blue eyes. (Gen)

Your story _____

• *Share an experience where you believed in someone despite suggestions that your hope was in vain.*

• *Was there ever a time when you felt "hope against all hope"? How did things turn out? How did you feel about it?*

Tante grazie!

It was going to be a great holiday for an American couple driving around Italy with their twelve-year-old son, Nicholas. Instead they were to return home without their beloved son.

On a stretch of freeway in a remote, mountainous area, a car of bandits pulled alongside the Americans and signaled them with a gun to pull over. When the father sped up, a bullet was fired into the back of the car. Nicholas, asleep on the back seat, received a bullet to his head and died hours later in hospital. Italians were shocked by the senseless crime, but even more amazed by the response of Nicholas' parents as they were interviewed on national television. They were upset and tearful but without a hint of bitterness and revenge. They readily agreed for Nicholas' organs to be used for urgently needed transplants, knowing that they would save the lives of people from the same country that had robbed their son of his life. "Our tragedy has been bad enough," they said. "At least this way other parents may be spared the grief of losing their child."

In fact, four lives were saved through transplants of a heart, liver, and kidneys. Three weeks later, a ten-year-old boy named Andreo smiled into the TV cameras as he left the hospital after receiving Nicholas' heart. Did he have any message for the American couple, he was asked in Italian? Andreo waved excitedly: "tante grazie!" (many thanks).

Your story

- *The story of the American couple's tragedy made a strong impression in Italy, a country with one of the lowest rates of organ donation in the western world. Several TV programs featured various people who pondered how these parents could have been so big-hearted. From where did they get their strength of character? How could they be so forgiving?*
- *What is your reaction to this story?*
- *Do you have a story to tell about someone who looked beyond their own pain and reached out to others?*

One night

My friend and I were in a café late one night when a man at the next table started to call out to us. He was drunk and his behavior irritating. I would have ignored him, but my friend had other ideas. I watched, fascinated, as she gently and lovingly drew him into conversation, getting to know his name and occupation, his outlook on life, the story of the breakdown of his marriage, and his attitude toward God.

An hour or so later, as the alcohol wore off and the coffee took effect, the man was visibly touched by my friend's listening ear and her gentle challenge to seek support from his local church. "Maybe I'll start talking to God again," he muttered, as their conversation drew to a close. (Donna)

Frank's story

"I am overwhelmed by the love of people," he said. "I didn't realize how much they cared. You could almost say it is a joy to die."

These words were spoken by a priest dying of cancer. Supported through his illness by loving friends, he had come to know, in a new way, that he was loved. He realized he was important to others not simply for what he did, but for who he was. For Frank, death was not the end but the beginning of a new experience of God's infinitely loving presence. (Frank Wallace, SJ, *What God Wants*, EJ Dywer, 1993)

Your story _____

- *"Hope is empowering and opens up new possibilities." Do you agree with this statement? Why or why not?*
- *Name some of the unique characteristics of Christian hope.*
- *How have you come to know that you are loved by others? by God?*

9

7) MARK 6:7-13
He began to send them out two by two

Summoned and sent

When our eldest son was finishing middle school, it seemed that he and his friends would be going to different high schools. We wanted them all to keep in contact with each other and also with the parish, so we offered our home as a gathering place on the fourth Friday of every month. The process we adopted was simple: the other parents would drop off and pick up their children, who would bring five dollars toward dinner—pizzas, hot dogs, chips, sodas, and the like. We would provide the entertainment—games, music, videos, or trivia quizzes. Some months we would meet at venues like a skating rink, a bowling alley, or a sports arena.

Word of the group quickly spread, and four other families soon followed our example and offered their homes to their children's friends. This means that for several years now we have had a home-based parish youth group of seventy-five or so young people operating effectively with little or no fuss.

One parent said to us recently: "I don't know what you do with them but our girls are always buzzing in the back seat when we drive them home." Our family, too, is always on a high at the end of these evenings. The kids are very happy to have us with them and to share in their fun. It is good, too, that they have adults other than their parents to relate to, an extended faith family, really.

Dealing with the adolescents on this basis has really given us a great sense of hope. These kids are just fantastic! (Kerry and John)

Your story _____

• *Jesus calls us to take the Good News into our world, to invite people to receive Christ into their hearts and lives. How have you been "called and sent"?*

• *Consider how the gifts of a friend may be needed in your local community, and invite this person to share their gifts.*

• *What is your own mission? Ask a friend to help you answer this.*

8) LUKE 1:1–4
So that you may know the truth concerning the things about which you have been instructed

A good news perspective

Our neighbors were having marital difficulties. Cultural tensions, financial strain, and two headstrong personalities made for a very volatile relationship. They had separated several times, but each time had decided to give the marriage another go.

When chatting with the wife, at first I simply empathized with her problems ("Gee, marriage can be tough, can't it?") and offered bits of advice. Then one day a fresh thought struck me which I instinctively voiced aloud. "What a love story!" I exclaimed. "You two have been through hell and high water, and here you are still committed to working at your marriage. That is an inspiring example of what love is all about!"

She smiled and didn't say much, but after that I noticed a subtle shift in our conversation. Instead of focusing on the obstacles, she talked about how she and her husband were working to resolve them. The struggles continued, but her whole attitude was more hope-filled.

Years later, not long after their twenty-fifth wedding anniversary, the wife took me aside and told me that my positive words had changed her whole perspective on their marriage. "When Dan and I were going through that difficult period, most of our friends were anticipating our divorce," she said. "I started to believe we were heading that way, too. But you were different. When you praised us for our 'love story,' you gave me hope. You believed in our marriage. And that made all the difference."
(RC)

Your story _____

- *How do pessimism and fear get in the way of your vision of life?*
- *What good news message do you think God would like to give you this day? What can you say or do to bring a good news message to somebody else?*

11

2

*Stories
of Grieving
and Healing*

9)

MARK 14:1—15:47
My God, my God, why have you forsaken me?

A letter from Tasmania

In April of 1996, a gunman opened fire on a group of tourists visiting a popular Australian tourist site at the prison ruins in Port Arthur, Tasmania. Thirty-five people were killed in all. This excerpt from a letter describes the scene shortly after the tragedy occurred.

It was somber to say the least. People were just walking around quietly. It was awful seeing the places where bullets had landed. The police had circled each spot with yellow spray paint; efforts had been made to cover them up with black paint, but it was painfully obvious. The café where most of the people died is surrounded by flowers and tributes, at least three feet wide. The place where the bus was parked had a few flowers too. And the spot where the mother and her two daughters were killed...it too was marked by flowers. It really sent shivers up my spine.

It was sort of nice to see people just stand there thinking or praying at the various spots. Not much was said as we passed each other, just a nod or a smile. It was quite eerie. We walked around some of the ruins and when you think about the convicts who had been there, you wonder if there was a tragedy back when the prison had been active that had equaled this one.

We have had a lot of extra work at school associated with Port Arthur. Children lost friends and some of the teens and young adults actually work down there. It has been pretty horrendous, but of course there has been the dose of goodness shown in many ways. There have been lots of tears, but it is wonderful to see the support the children have given to each other, too. (Paula)

Your story

- *What is your reaction when you read about this and other tragic events? What do you think can be done—if anything—about this type of violent occurrence?*
- *Have you ever grieved with someone over a very deep loss? What was this like for you? What helped? What hindered? Where was God in your pain?*
- *Why is it important to mourn a great loss, whether private or public?*

10) MARK 6:30–34
He had compassion for them

A different kind of gig

Here, a musician speaks of a different kind of "gig" (engagement), when just the act of celebration was an act of survival and, ultimately, a decision to love.

It was a difficult gig, an emotional gig, different from any kind of performance we had ever done. On the surface everything looked typical: a community organization wanted our band for its annual fundraising dinner dance. The only difference? The organization was a support group for the families of murder victims and the money being raised was for a support house for people in similar situations.

Meeting many of the guests triggered memories of media headlines. Gross acts of violence—once reported on a distant TV screen or the front page of the newspaper—suddenly became larger than life as I was introduced to a victim's mother or father, sister or brother-in-law.

The whole body language of the audience was different, too. Even as they entered into the celebrations of the evening, the weight of their trauma was only thinly disguised. From the stage you could tell that people were at different phases of grieving, from the couple in sheer survival mode who could barely meet each other's eyes to those who had been walking the path of recovery for three years, seven years, ten years.

I came away from this experience with untold admiration and respect for these people. I mean, here were families at the lowest point of their lives, when probably all they felt like doing was giving up on life. Yet they chose to be there at a fundraising evening; they chose to do something to help other people. They chose not to allow their own pain to eclipse that deeply human spark of compassion and hope. (Mick)

Your story _____

• *Have you ever been in a situation such as the one described above? How did you get through it?*

• *Think of a time when you went beyond yourself to ease the burden of another. How was Christ present in that situation?*

• *How is Christ's love calling you to go beyond yourself today?*

11) MATTHEW 26:14—27:66
They came upon a man from Cyrene named Simon; they compelled this man to carry Jesus' cross

He carried me

When I was eight years old, I had an infection in my hip that caused me great pain. I couldn't walk—in fact, I could barely move—without crying out in agony. Dad took me to the hospital himself, and I can remember how distressed he was as he carried me to the car, knowing that by helping me he was also causing me physical suffering.

By the time we arrived at the hospital, my pain had grown to excruciating levels. As Dad helped me out of the car, I remember him saying to me with tears in his eyes: "Son, you're going to have to work with me here." Together we devised a way for him to transport me. I had my arms around his neck and was straddling him at a certain angle as he gently carried me into the hospital. So well did we work together that when a wheelchair was finally offered, I declined. It was easier on both of us for Dad to continue carrying me to the observation room.

As I tell this story today, I am forty years old. But I will always remember this incident. To me, it is like a little parable about how God helps us through our hurts. Like a loving parent, God feels every stab of our pain, and will do anything to help us. But sometimes we have to work with God and trust that together we will make it through the difficult journey. (Dan)

Your story _____

• *Describe a painful journey you have made through life. How was God present, or seemingly absent?*
• *Was there ever a time when you were able to help someone else through a painful time? What did you learn from this experience?*
• *What would you share from your own experience with someone who is suffering?*

12) LUKE 24:13-35
The Lord has risen indeed

The lunch

It was now six years since Helen broke off the engagement, six years since she had found out—one month before her intended marriage—that her fiancé had been having an affair with her best friend. Six years later, almost to the day, we were sitting in a restaurant looking back over that traumatic time. As a friend of Helen's family living in another town, I had heard of her suffering but had never spoken about it with Helen; until now.

I must confess to dreading this lunch. The night before I had visions of a bitter survivor clutching a voodoo doll. But the reality was even more incredible. There before me sat a healthy, happy woman enjoying a superb dish of pasta. I was astonished at Helen's obvious contentment as she talked about her life. She told me that, after walking around in a devastated, zombie-like state for two years following the betrayal, her enthusiasm for life had gradually returned and she had emerged stronger than ever. "In a way, I'm glad it happened," she told me. "I understand so much more about myself, about life…and I talk to God a lot more, too." After the shock, the anger, and the state of simply getting through the day had somewhat abated, the healing slowly came.

For Helen it was a gradual realization and appreciation of her own God-given self-worth that pulled her through. As for her ex-fiancé and ex-best friend, she wished them well and harbored no envy for their relationship. "I'm looking for a relationship built on trust," she said with determination. It was inspiring to listen to her. In fact, I learned a lot during that lunch, and felt both happy and moved by her journey. Out of the worst scenario, Helen had emerged victorious as a loving human being. I would not wish such trauma on anyone. But yes, in some sense, I was glad it happened too. (Claire)

Your story _____

* *What is your favorite story of new life, of how good came from trauma? Perhaps your story is about a birth or a healing, a new lease on life or a joyful celebration, or a glimmer of hope in a dark situation.*

Dad

I look at his photo now and I realize how much I love and adore him. He was a truly great man; one of the most beautiful human beings who ever walked the earth. He commanded respect, yet he never got angry. When we were kids, if we acted up Mom would say, "Wait till your father gets home!" But when he did he would just talk to us in a manner which won our respect. He had that way about him, always calm and understanding of people. In fact, he never had a bad word to say about anybody.

Dad had a great sense of fairness. I remember as a teenager, making a fuss about the fact that he would go watch my brothers play football, but he had never come to watch me play soccer. "It's not fair!" I said. So the following week, Dad turned up at my game. I'll never forget the feeling I had seeing him arrive to watch me. It meant so much. After that, he kept coming, week after week. Deep down I felt worthy; I was important enough for my Dad to be there.

He had a great sense of humor, my Dad, and sensational looks (which we used to kid him about!). But most of all he had guts. Like the way he handled cancer. He never once felt sorry for himself. And that is amazing when I think of how much he had to live for. He was the picture of fitness, heavily into sports, and a bit of a legend in the town as a player, captain, and coach.

He was only in his fifties when he died and there were a number of newspaper articles written about him. Invariably they ended up praising him not just for his athletic prowess but for his goodness as a truly Christian person. (Fiona)

Your story

- *Recall a time when you were "hungry" or "thirsty": who fed you?*
- *In your everyday life, how are you able to feed the hungry and give drink to the thirsty?*
- *What is your idea of judgment day? What will it be like?*

14) Matthew 25:1–13
Keep awake therefore, for you know neither the day nor the hour

Together again

It had not been a great year for our family. A lot had gone wrong, events we could not have predicted and which we would find it difficult to recover from.

I will always remember that Christmas when we all were able to get together for the holiday. It was the first time we had been together since the funerals and wakes and terrible phone calls that had marked the previous twelve months. At first, we simply went through the motions of festivity. Gradually, we became close again, just like we needed to.

This will always remain in my memory as a strong Christmas, a time when we appreciated each other and celebrated being family. (LK)

A friend in need

At a time when our family was coping with the death of a family member, a neighbor turned up on our doorstep with a home-cooked dinner. No fuss. No invasion of privacy. Just a brief, warm, one-minute visit while she dropped off a casserole. We appreciated not just the practical help, but the knowledge that somebody cared. It was her way of being present to us in our suffering. (Brigid)

Your story _____

- *Describe an experience when a time of family crisis was also a time of grace or opportunity.*
- *In what area does your family most need God's healing presence at this point in time?*
- *What do you appreciate most about your family?*
- *What heartfelt prayer would you like to offer for your family?*

19

15) JOHN 18:1—19:42
He said to the disciple, "Here is your mother"; from that hour the disciple took her into his own home

Take time

A nurse says: "There is a lady in our nursing home who is 102 years old. Whenever she speaks it is always connected with the day, forty-five years ago, that her husband dropped dead in front of her. If I greet her with, 'Isn't it a lovely day!' she'll say, 'He just died... there was nothing I could do.' I realize she needs to grieve and I try to give her time, but there is so little I can do for her under the constraints of work schedules. I am painfully aware that if this woman had had the opportunity to talk and grieve her loss forty-five years ago, she would be so much more at peace today.

"There are just some things which need to be addressed in the present moment. If we put them off until tomorrow or next year, it may be too late." (KGP)

Saying goodbye

As a grief counselor, I am all too aware that the death of a loved one can be a very "busy" time. There can be so many details to attend to: contacting relatives, organizing the funeral, writing an obituary, signing medical and insurance statements. In the midst of it all, grieving people can all too often find their grief shoved aside for the sake of the business at hand.

I think people need to realize how important it is for the bereaved person to spend time with the body of the deceased person. An important part of the healing process is to say goodbye; to "be" with their loved one. (TS)

Your story _____

- *Describe a time when you shared another person's grief. What did you say, or not say? What did you do, or not do?*
- *How did it feel being in this situation? What did you learn through this experience?*

16) LUKE 17:11-19
One of them, when he saw that he was healed, turned back, praising God with a loud voice

Healing touch

I was having dinner with a group of friends at a crowded restaurant in town. Despite the congenial atmosphere, I felt removed from everyone in the room. My friends were living it up, enjoying the food and conversation; but I did not feel part of the festivities. Suddenly I started to cry: ridiculously, irrationally. What made it worse was that no one noticed I was crying! I felt completely alone. In desperation I ran out of the restaurant, stumbled into a back alley, and just let the tears flow. I can't really say why I cried, I just did.

Now the restaurant was near a very rough part of town, and this back alley was not the place to be crying irrationally at night with no one around. Nevertheless, I kept crying while sitting on the edge of the pavement with my head between my knees.

Suddenly a hand touched my shoulder and a man's voice came out of the night: "Are you all right?"

I should have been startled. I should have offered him my wallet immediately. Instead, I instinctively knew I was safe. I said, "Yeah, thanks, I'm fine. I just can't stop crying!" With that he smiled and disappeared into the shadows.

For the first time that night I felt I was not alone. (Mark)

A cry for help

"My parents hate me," said the teenage girl to the guidance counselor.

"How do you know they hate you?"

"Because they let me do whatever I want."

Your story _____

• *Social alienation is a common ailment in our society. Has there ever been a time when you felt like a "leper"?*

• *Who do you know who may feel alienated, either from the church or from your community? How can you reach out to them?*

21

3

*Stories
of
Forgiveness*

17) LUKE 6:27–38
Love your enemies, do good to those who hate you

Maria's choice

This story comes from a Marist Center in the Philippines which cares for homeless boys. The Center is called Balay Pasilungan, *which translates as "House of Shelter."*

I had not been working long at Balay Pasilungan when Maria, who was studying to be a social worker, arrived. I first explained to her the Center's procedures. Then, I looked around at the forty boys in front of me, and randomly selected three for her to work with. After an hour she came back looking rather flushed. I assumed that this was her first real experience working with very poor children, and I sought to console her.

Maria told me that the first boy she interviewed could not be reunited with his father as his father was in prison for murder. I explained to her that a number of the children were on the streets because their parents were in prison, and not to let it upset her too much. "Yes," replied Maria. "But I have just discovered that the man his father murdered was my own father!"

After we both recovered slightly from the shock I suggested that perhaps she might like to leave Balay Pasilungan or, at the very least, work with another boy.

"I am social worker," replied Maria. "And I am also a Christian. It is not this boy's fault that his father killed my father. I would like to help him as much as I can." (PC, courtesy *Marist Newsletter*, June 1994 , Vol. 45, No. 2)

Your story _____

- *Ask yourself: What would I have done in Maria's shoes?*
- *Who is the most forgiving person you know? Why is this so?*
- *Who in your life now might you need to forgive?*
- *In what ways do you need to be forgiven?*
- *What is one practical step you can take this week toward forgiveness, whether of yourself or of someone else?*

18) Matthew 18:15–20

Truly I tell you, whatever you bind on earth will be bound in heaven, and whatever you loose on earth will be loosed in heaven.

Sarah's story

When Sarah was nine years old, she walked in on her mother as she was about to attempt suicide. Twenty-five years later, Sarah says she can still see the scene as clear as day: the garage…the noose…her mother standing on a box. "I screamed and screamed until my father came running. It was a moment of sheer terror. But it was also a terror familiar to me. Mom had been talking about suicide for a while, as she was suffering from some kind of mental breakdown. I lived in fear at the thought that my mother might kill herself. Then, when it actually appeared it might happen…."

While Sarah's family managed to pull through that traumatic time and reestablish a stable family life, Sarah says the incident has left her with some painful scars. "Even now my mother's attempted suicide haunts me in relationships. I get 'clingy,' and say: 'Where are you going? What time will you be home?' It's as if part of me is saying, 'Don't leave me!' For a long time I was very resentful towards Mom for all she had put us through. But over the years something has shifted inside me, and I feel differently about the whole situation."

That shift is evident in the way Sarah speaks. Instead of bitterness there is a peace, an acceptance, a gentleness that suggests a deeper well of love and forgiveness. "There came a point where I made the decision to let go of my anger. As I have gone through life, I have been through some pretty tough times myself. It has given me some insight into what Mom must have been going through. I can now say, 'It's okay, Mom. I understand. You had all those pressures. It was a tough time for you.' And I know that she really does love us."

Your story

- *Forgiveness is freeing: would you agree?*
- *Describe a situation or event from your childhood which you understand differently as an adult. Why did your feelings change?*
- *Is there a rift with a family member which is in need of repair? This week, look for the goodness in a person you find hard to love.*

Never too late

When I was growing up, the couple living next door had a lot of marital problems. They struggled to stay together for many years, but finally the husband's alcoholism just got too much for the wife and she left him. After that, I heard he went downhill with his alcohol problem, and ended up living on the streets. Meanwhile, his wife got on with her life and filed for a divorce. I presumed that was the tragic end of the relationship and never thought much more of it.

Many years later I was astounded to hear they were back together again. He was dying of cirrhosis of the liver and she had taken him in to care for him. She nursed him until the day he died.

I have never forgotten this couple, and I retell their story to my own children. This relationship, which I was tempted to write off as a hopeless case, has in fact taught me a great lesson of the power and possibilities of forgiveness. (George)

Simply loving

One of the most extraordinary acts of forgiveness I have ever heard concerned a woman who quietly admitted to me that each week at Mass she prays for the woman who had an affair with her fiancé. "I feel sorry for her," was the way she put it, without a trace of malice. "Everyone lost out during that painful chapter in our lives. She went through hell, too." (Carol)

Your story

- *Who do you find hardest to forgive?*
- *Why do you think forgiveness can be so difficult? What gets in the way?*
- *How can we make forgiveness a lifetime habit?*

20) JOHN 15:9–17
Love one another as I have loved you

Together forever

I have a childhood memory of my parents standing in the kitchen, exchanging sharp words. Suddenly, my father broke through the tension and went up to Mom. He tapped her gently on the arm, saying expectantly, "Hey, tell me something...tell me something...." Reluctantly, Mom's scowl relaxed into a half-smile before volunteering her half of the equation. "I love you," she said, and they embraced.

I gradually learned that this little exchange, repeated again and again over forty-two years of marriage, symbolized for them a powerful decision: no issue is so big that we will ever allow it to come between our love for one another. (Vincent)

Shift of the heart

"Grandma! Here's a lovely plate! Grandma...oops." Crash...shriek... wail. Granddaughter number five, four years old and only-trying-to-help, had just dropped grandma's treasured heirloom. The fact that it had been in the family for one hundred years and now lay in jagged pieces was enough to send tears streaming down grandma's face. Yet at the same moment she was cuddling the equally distraught four-year-old. "It's okay darling, I know you didn't mean any harm."

In this crazy mixture of tears and love I saw a simple but vital gospel message communicated: people are more important than things. No heirloom is more important than the love it symbolizes. (ML)

Your story _____

- *Name some of the "little things" that can make or break a relationship.*
- *What are some important expressions of unconditional love in your family? in your parish? in your community?*

21) Matthew 11:25–30

Take my yoke upon you, and learn from me; for I am gentle and humble in heart, and you will find rest for your souls

Tracy

When my roommate moved in, my first impression was: "This woman cannot be for real!" At twenty-three, Tracy seemed the embodiment of selfless love. She never had a bad word for anyone. If someone wronged her she patiently excused their behavior. In my cynicism, I labeled her as naive, the product of a sheltered religious upbringing.

That was before I met her father, and the truth dawned. Tracy was no stranger to the school of hard knocks. In fact, she had grown up in an abusive household. Her father, an obsessive personality, did not know what it meant to talk: he could only shout. From early on, this beautiful, intelligent, and faithful young woman had been continually told that she was ugly, stupid, and a financial burden.

Shocked and dismayed by this revelation, I asked Tracy how she came to be so free of bitterness in the face of her upbringing. She winced and was silent for a long while, pondering this painful topic. "My sister became bitter," she said at last. "I started to go that way too. But then, at sixteen, I made a huge decision: to forgive Dad every day. I think that's what has made the difference. And it is impossible to do so without prayer. I pray every day for a forgiving heart."

Tracy is currently taking Saturday morning classes in German, the language of her father's country of birth. The reason? "I know Dad's heritage means a lot to him," she says. "It might help open up the lines of communication between us."

Your story

- *Sometimes forgiveness takes time, especially in a relationship where the hurts runs deep. How does this apply to a situation in your life?*
- *How can you work at mending the breaks in such a relationship?*
- *Try building into your daily routine a short prayer for a forgiving heart.*

22) LUKE 18:9–14
All who exalt themselves will be humbled, but all who humble themselves will be exalted

The big chill

We've all experienced it, especially married couples: the icy stares…the cold silence…the crisp, one-word answers which say, "I am really angry with you!" The awful thing is that you want to stay angry—at least until the other has made amends, apologized sufficiently, reversed whatever it was that caused the tension, or completely changed their personality!

But of course, that is not the way to solve a conflict. At least, that is what we have discovered during our thirty-seven years of married life! Harboring grudges and insisting that the other change may have made us feel self-righteous, but it has never brought us closer together.

So there comes a time to make a decision: will I keep sulking or will I make the first move toward peace? Reason tells you "It's not fair!" Having to make a choice can be infuriating, but the fact is, a choice must be made.

So you decide to let go of "I'm right, you're wrong," and focus on the relationship. You offer a cup of coffee or a hug. You turn your scowl into a hesitant smile that says, "This fight is really silly, isn't it?" And little by little the big freeze starts to melt. Communication becomes possible. Issues take on a new perspective. Solutions have a real chance. But only because you have put the bond of love first, above everything.

In every conflict, somebody has to make the first move toward reconciliation. And that somebody might as well be me. (MP)

Your story _____

- *Think of a situation where tension between two or more people was handled in an appropriate way. What key principles were operating?*
- *What can married couples teach the wider community about handling conflict?*

23) MATTHEW 28:1–10
He is not here; for he has been raised, as he said

A new day

God's love is relentless and always an invitation to love again, to believe again, to start afresh.

Our first years of marriage were very difficult—so full of suffering. Although we came from superficially similar backgrounds, there were vast differences in our individual family experiences. We had learned to relate to people in totally different ways, ranging from trust and openness to defensiveness and suspicion. You can imagine the communication problems we had! It seemed as if everything we said was misunderstood by the other.

Our life together went downhill to the extent that we finally separated. We found that, by ourselves, we had neither the strength nor the wisdom to change things, although we tried every avenue of help, including counseling.

The turning point for us began with the example of other families who helped us understand how to pick up the pieces and come together again as a married couple. These friends from the Focolare movement listened to us for hours on end. They showed us how to live those words of the gospel that teach us how to love one another, how to forgive. They helped us to see the positive rather than the negative.

Now we are back together again. The problems haven't disappeared altogether, but we have learned that we can always start again. We each really try to see the other as a new person every day. Through our efforts and perseverance in continuing to love, both in those years of suffering and now as well, we have discovered a joy and peace in our lives beyond anything we could ever have imagined. (JB; courtesy *The World of Families*, Focolare Movement, 1994)

Your story

- *What life-giving moments and memories are you helping to create in your family? in your parish? in your neighborhood?*
- *Where do you see the risen Christ in your day-to-day life?*

24) JOHN 20:19–31
Jesus came and stood among them and said, "Peace be with you"

Peace be with you!

I hadn't seen my grandmother for months, and boy, was I feeling guilty! The crazy thing was that the less I visited, the more guilty I felt… and the less I felt I could look her in the eye! I would postpone my visit yet again.

Well, I finally went up to her door one day, bracing myself for a well-deserved look of disapproval. But I had completely misjudged the woman. As I walked in, she greeted me with sincere warmth. "Why hello there! How lovely to see you!" Not an ounce of resentment. Not a drop of "Where have you been?" In that one forgiving gesture I felt peace and gratitude flood through my being. Suddenly I wanted to visit her!

A forgiving attitude: what a powerful way to set each other free. (Joseph)

Presence

Not many people knew the man was dying of AIDS. To most he was simply a enthusiastic newcomer to the parish, always the first to arrive and the last to leave a parish function. As he had little family and few friends, the parish was fast becoming his home.

As his disease set in and he lost his mobility and coherence, a number of his fellow parishioners became a faithful, quiet presence to him. When he died, two of these parishioners discovered that they had been named as his next of kin.

At the end of his life, he had found peace and a sense of community.

Your story _____

• *Describe a time when you felt forgiven and at peace. What was said or done? What impact did it have on you? What did you learn from this experience?*

31

4

Stories of Faith

25)

Beyond fear

When I was sixteen weeks pregnant, my husband, Robert, and I found out that our baby had encephalocoele, a form of neural tube defect. Our doctor at that time told us that our baby would not survive the full term of the pregnancy, and if by some miracle did survive, would have severe physical and mental disabilities. His solution was an abortion or, as it was politely put, "termination" of the pregnancy. I could not get out of his office fast enough.

Initially, Robert and I were grief-stricken. We hugged each other, cried with each other, and talked about what we were feeling, which was predominantly fear: could we handle what lay ahead? We felt isolated from everyone, and at times, even from each other, yet we were closer than we had ever been.

Our beautiful little boy, Jacob, is now nearly six months old. Jacob was born with only one eye, one ear, a cleft palate and harelip, and major heart problems. Thank God, however, all we really noticed was that his hair was red! That surprised us more than anything else and was the cause of much joy and laughter at Jacob's birth.

Jacob is our inspiration and joy. We have never seen a more beautiful baby and if we only kiss him a million times a day, it is never enough. Our little angel is definitely not brain dead; he is an alert little baby. We take each day as it comes and treasure each moment that we have. We marvel at the things he does that other parents may take for granted. We place Jacob in God's generous, yet strong hands.

I have been so blessed with the gifts of an amazing and courageous husband, a beautiful little boy, a wonderful family, and good friends. (Carmel; first published in *Troubadour*, Summer 1995)

Your story

- *Describe a time when you experienced inner calm and strength amid external turmoil. What was the source of your strength?*
- *What does it mean to trust people? to trust God?*
- *How do you nourish your faith?*

26) MATTHEW 20:1–16
Take what belongs to you and go; I choose to give to this last the same as I give to you

Two women

The scene: two women friends are chatting about life, love, and God. One has stayed committed to the faith and traditions of her Catholic community since the cradle. The other is a "late arrival" to the practice of her faith. Having walked away from the church for many years, she has only recently returned in response to a profound experience of conversion and reconciliation. Their conversation goes something like this:

Cradle Catholic: Your zeal for the faith is amazing. It makes me feel old and tired! The pews are full of people like me. We are so committed but in many ways we are simply going through the motions. We have lost that fire of conversion.

Returning Catholic: Your constancy is what amazes me. Don't forget that it is only because all you "tired old Catholics" are still here that I have a church to come back to!

Cradle Catholic: Your enthusiasm is a refreshing. It challenges us.

Returning Catholic: Your commitment is challenging. It is all very well to be on fire with faith, but now I have to ask myself: can I hang in there for the long haul?

Cradle Catholic: Sometimes I feel a little envious of your newfound faith. I mean, it seems like you go off and "live it up" for twenty years and then God showers you with blessings!

Returning Catholic: But I also have to live with the things I have done. There are heartaches here which you have been spared because you chose differently.

Your story

- *With whom do you most identify in the above conversation?*
- *Read the parable cited above. What is your feeling about this story?*
- *God's ways are not our ways. How do you struggle with this reality in your own life? Pray for a generous spirit.*

27) JOHN 21:1–19

Jesus said to Simon Peter, "Simon son of John, do you love me more than these?" He said to him, "Yes, Lord; you know that I love you"

Believe!

While Mom had been suffering from chronic heart failure for some time, the family took it for granted that she would be around indefinitely. When I received the news that she had died, it was a strange sensation. Nothing mattered except the fact that she was dead. All the normal reference points disappeared, to be replaced by the central realization that what had been the most important referent—Mom—was now a memory without a physical or geographic location. It was an unexpected sense of being orphaned, of being cut loose from my moorings at the age of fifty-four, of having lost the one who had always been an absolute. I felt a profound grief from deep inside, not just from behind the eyes as seen in the movies.

Through this all, my experience of faith was different, too. It went beyond feeling "sadder but wiser" to hit at the core of things. For me, the question was: do I have any faith at all, or is what appears to be my beliefs simply the echo of Mom and Dad's faith? As long as my parents were alive, faith by proxy was possible. We could afford to half-jokingly indulge Mom's all-encompassing faith: she had enough for all of us.

But suddenly, when you are on your own, watch out! There is a huge void with nothing to fill it but your own faith. At the funeral, we read this passage from Paul's first letter to the Corinthians: "And now faith, hope, and love abide, these three; and the greatest of these is love" (1 Corinthians 13:13).

Although the foundations of my faith have been shaken, I know in my heart that I have the surety of Mom's love, beckoning me to believe, to have faith like hers. (Paul)

Your story _____

- *Have you made a journey from doubt to faith in your own life?*
- *What makes it hard for you to have faith? How do you overcome your doubts?*
- *Who or what helps to strengthen your convictions?*

28) JOHN 4:5–42

The water that I will give will become in them a spring of water gushing up to eternal life

Wellsprings of faith

This story took place in a two-bed hospital room.

Both myself and Mary, the woman in the other bed, were seriously ill. It didn't take long before we were chatting, relating our life stories to one another. Our bond was forged partly by the discovery that we both shared a deep faith in God.

Mary was happily married, had two grownup daughters and a ten-year-old son named Danny. It was obvious to me that Danny was the apple of her eye. The many little incidents she related left no doubt in my mind that mother and son were very close.

One day, flowers started to arrive at Mary's end of the room. More flowers came, and still more, so that soon I was enjoying the floral overflow on my side of the room. "Why Mary!" I exclaimed. "Is it your birthday?" She looked me straight in the eye and said, "No, it's not my birthday. I have just been told I have five weeks to live."

As soon as I could recover my equilibrium, I spoke words of comfort. Through our gentle sharings, our bond of faith was deepened still further. Among other things, I said, "It must be so hard to leave Danny." She looked at me and said, "God must have other plans for Danny."

I choked back my tears in the face of such courage, thanking God for the gift of this woman, and asking that, in my own hour of need, I too might draw deeply on the living water of my faith. (Angela)

Your story

• *Describe a person who draws from a deep well of faith as they face life's challenges. What does this person say or do that impresses you?*

• *From what "well" do you draw living water?*

37

29) MATTHEW 24:37–44
Keep awake therefore, for you do not know on what day your Lord is coming

Margy

Margy's beeper went off as I was sitting next to her at a parish gathering. She shifted the tubes that connected her to her portable oxygen tank, leaned over, and calmly said, "Do you know where I can find the nearest phone?" The beeper meant one of two things: either she was being summoned for a transplant—the result of a three-year wait—or the beeper had gone off accidentally. Her friends gathered and began to pray as Margy went to call the hospital. It turned out to be a false alarm.

Recalling this incident later, I pondered the maturity of faith of this extraordinary woman. Margy could be called for surgery at any time. The success of the operation was not guaranteed. On one hand, it might be the gateway to a new life. On the other hand, it might worsen her condition even to the point of death.

The decision to enter such a scheme requires enormous strength of character. Margy lives each day in faith. Peacefully and matter-of-factly she goes about her business; waiting, hoping, longing for the tangible gift of full health, yet knowing that the fulfillment of God's promise to her might be to meet the Lord face-to-face. Either way, when that beeper goes off, Margy is ready. (TP)

Letter of life

After battling four horrendous years of post-natal depression, a young mother, now emerging from the ordeal wrote to a friend: "Not a day goes past without me wondering in awe at the sky and the flowers and thanking God for seeing me and my family through my darkest hours."

Your story _____

- *How does the gift of hope get you through tough times?*
- *Is there a likely scenario in your own future which you'd rather not think about (e.g., the possibility of losing your job or losing someone you love)? How "prepared" are you to deal with such an event?*
- *Name ten things in your life for which you are grateful.*

Inside cover

I asked a friend if I could borrow his Bible. What I did not expect was to be handed such a battered, stained, and obviously well-used treasure. On the inside cover were eight addresses, beginning with a home address in the scrawled handwriting of a child, to the addresses of various overseas institutions where my friend had studied and taught, to the business address of his current job.

Knowing a little of the ups and downs of this man's life, it occurred to me that some of these addresses represented tough times. They say the Word of God sustains us throughout our lives. I was holding a symbol of that truth: a Bible that had been everywhere with my friend. From boyhood to manhood, from Australia to Europe, in good times and sorrow, it was the sign of a faithful man.

Rocky ground

A man was charged with several horrific murders. At the end of his trial at which relatives of the victims were distraught with grief and anger, he was found guilty and sentenced to life imprisonment.

In his brief public response before the court, this convicted murderer made an extraordinary statement. He said, "I should have stayed with God. But I didn't. And now I have caused this holocaust."

Your story _____

- *What are the "rocks, thorns, and weeds" that get in the way of you hearing and responding to the Word of God?*
- *What attitudes and daily habits help to enrich the "good soil" in your life?*

31) MARK 1:12–15

The time is fulfilled, and the kingdom of God has come near; repent, and believe in the good news

Sid

I don't remember my godfather. He was my Uncle Sid and he died of cancer when I was one and a half years old. Even so, he has had a huge impact on my faith. Mom told me that Sid, bedridden and fast deteriorating, had promised her he would not die until he could see that I could walk myself to Mass.

It makes me feel humble yet empowered that my godfather, terminally ill and suffering considerable physical discomfort, should still be so concerned about my faith. There have been many times over the years when I have not felt like going to Mass. But then I think of Sid's faith in me that when I could walk, I would get to Mass. It always gets me there. (JF)

Courage!

It was my first stint as a catechist. I had been given a class of high school freshman to teach. I was twenty-five, inexperienced, and scared! I was afraid of losing control of the class. I was afraid of failing at my task. I was afraid of a lot of things.

In my anxiety I turned to Jesus in prayer. Gradually, my focus began to change. My thoughts became less preoccupied with myself and more focused on the students. A phrase kept recurring within me: the most important thing is to love them. In this realization I experienced a quiet, reassuring strength and peace. (Vince)

Your story _____

- *Name some key people who have passed on the faith to you. What did they say or do that had an impact?*
- *Describe a crossroad in your life where you consciously chose a particular value system.*

32) MARK 14:12–16, 22–26
This is my body...this is my blood of the covenant

A witness of love

Recently, a missionary sister serving in Sudan told us stories about her life and work. She ministers in a very poor village which has no permanent dwellings and many refugees.

One story I found compelling was about of a young disabled boy who could not walk but who determinedly crawled to Mass every day. On one occasion he asked this Sister if she could find him a pair of thongs. She could not understand why a boy who could not walk would want a pair of thongs until she realized they were not for his feet but for his hands. The thongs would offer some protection on his daily journey to Mass.

Listening to this unassuming religious sister speak so matter-of-factly about her ministry, I was struck by her generosity of spirit and quiet sacrifice. Here she is, a woman the age of my grandmother, choosing to live in harsh conditions, miles away from family and worldly comforts. And why? Because it is her way of witnessing to Jesus' love. (Anthony)

That much

Two-year-old Luke and I often play a little game. I ask how much he loves me and he stretches out his arms and says "This much!"

We were at church one Sunday. Luke noticed the crucifix over the altar, which was a very prominent piece of modern art. "Look, Mommy," he said. "Jesus is saying, 'This much!'" and he stretched out his arms. I laughed at his cuteness, glad that he recognized the figure to be Jesus. I felt a lump in my throat as I said, "Yes, Luke, that is what Jesus is saying. He loves us that much." (RC)

Your story _____

• *Think of somebody you love. How do you show them that you care? What joys and sorrows have been part of that caring?*
• *How have you experienced Jesus' love in times of great joy? In times of great stress? In the ordinary, mundane events of life?*

5

*Stories
about Tough
Decisions*

33) JOHN 3:14–21
Those who do what is true come to the light, so that it may be clearly seen that their deeds have been done in God

Wrestling with the truth

My brother Brendan is a big guy. His six-foot-something muscular frame and shaved scalp make him a formidable presence as he leans over the pool table and sinks another billiard ball. "I'm not joking, man," he says to me. "Pretty soon I'm going to have to make a decision. I'm either going to ditch this religion thing, or else I'm going to say 'Okay, I'll quit my job.'"

The contradiction of trying to live out his Catholic values while working as a bouncer in one of the city's seediest nightclubs is starting to get to Brendan. Given the circles he mixes in I marvel that, at twenty-five, he has managed to stay faithful to his religion for this long. But then Brendan has always had a deep down loyalty to his Catholic upbringing. Perhaps that is why, as part of his job, he will confiscate drugs and flush them down the toilet instead of offering them for resale. And he disappoints his girlfriend because he refuses to sleep with her, saying, "It's just not right; marriage is for keeps." Eventually, our environment does affect us. And judging by his comments, Brendan is starting to feel the tension.

God, how I love my brother! I pray and yearn for him as he wrestles with the choices confronting him…choices that only he can make. (Vince)

Your story _____

• *What contradictions do you experience between your faith and your day-to-day life?*
• *Reflect on what it is like to wrestle with sin, even as you strive for goodness. What helps you stay focused?*

34) Mark 7:1–8,14–15,21–23

This people honors me with their lips, but their hearts are far from me

Let's do coffee

One lovely, lazy Sunday morning, I decided to stop off at a coffee shop after Mass and read the newspaper. No sooner was I perched happily over a steaming cappuccino, relishing the inspiring feelings that I had enjoyed at Mass, than God threw me a whammy. Through the window of the café I could see the humped shape of a man crouched in a doorway, a cigarette dangling limply from the corner of his mouth. He was obviously a homeless alcoholic, and it was a sad sight.

The challenge of the morning's homily was beginning to gnaw at my conscience. Would you believe that I sat there for twenty minutes trying to pluck up the courage to respond? All I wanted to do was buy the man a cup of coffee as a simple gesture of caring. But for twenty minutes I agonized over the decision. Was it token charity? Would he reject me? Was I being patronizing? What would Jesus do? What would people think?

With my heart in my mouth, I made my move. "Excuse me, sir…."
"What?!" he barked.

"You look like a man who could use a strong cup of coffee. Can I buy you one?" He stared at me suspiciously before saying, "Yeah."

I went back inside the cafe and returned with a cup of coffee and a sandwich. "Got any sugars?" he muttered.

I dutifully retrieved the sugar, mumbled some good wishes…and fled! My heart was pumping. I was shocked to realize the extent of my own unease. Why was it so hard to be a little bit neighborly to a fellow human being? (MG)

Your story

• *When was the last time you had a crisis of conscience? Describe the crisis. How did you resolve it?*
• *Recall a difficult decision you had to make. Would you make the same choice again?*

35) Luke 10:38–42
You are worried and distracted by many things; there is need of only one thing

The day we never had

She was a girl with a slight intellectual disability who was also a severe epileptic. Throughout grammar school she had been my friend. We sat next to each other in class, ate at the same lunch table, and sometimes did homework together after school. I knew what to do if she had a seizure.

Despite her disabilities, which included a pronounced stutter that made conversation difficult, she was wonderful company. Looking back, I see our friendship as an enriching experience. Her air of optimism affected me deeply. Her liveliness and spirit were amazing.

Her family moved to another part of the country right before high school began, and I did not see her for five or so years when one day she called me, right out of the blue. She simply wanted to meet me to talk and catch up with each other's lives. She was offering friendship after all these years of being apart.

To my eternal regret, I made up an excuse about being too busy and declined her invitation. My life was moving ahead in the fast lane, and I did not want to be slowed down by my friend's pace. To this day my rejection haunts me; not only for how I let her down but also for the experience I missed. After all this time, I still remember her energy and simple happiness, while whatever I was doing at the time of her call are long forgotten. I miss the day we never had. (Kim)

Your story _____

- *How do you decide between what is important and what is not?*
- *Draw up a list of this week's priorities. Then reflect on your list during prayer, perhaps while reading today's gospel. See if any of your priorities change.*
- *How is it possible to find time for God amid a busy schedule?*

What price freedom?

A Hungarian woman tells this story of her family's escape during the Communist suppression of the 1956 Hungarian uprising.

As the Russian tanks rolled past our home day after day, we knew the revolution had failed. I was 13 at the time. My mother was recently widowed. My older brother was in hiding. His revolutionary activities would have meant sure execution, so my mother made a decision that we would leave the country.

So one day we just walked out of our home with nothing but the clothes we wore, knowing we would never return. With my younger brother, sisters, and baby niece, there were six of us. We headed by train to a town near the border. We departed the train at midnight and my mother asked a man for directions. The man warned us not to go into the town as the Russians now had control of it. Instead he directed us to follow the train tracks that would take us to another town. We walked for some hours before seeking shelter at a house.

The following night, at about 2:00 AM, we made our way to the border. This was the most terrifying part of our journey. We had to walk through cornfields in the dark, fearful of being captured and shot (we could hear guard dogs barking), fearful of being blown to bits (the area was full of mines). My mother had sedated the baby so she would not cry. Somehow we made it across the border, unnoticed and unharmed. I recall crossing a bridge and knowing we were in Austria. It was not until much later, however, that the fear gave way to relief. We were free!

To this day I am in awe of the courage of my mother. She risked everything to bring us all to freedom. (Eniko)

Your story

- *What reactions do you have to Eniko's story? Have you, or do you know anyone who has ever had a similar experience?*
- *For whom or what would you be prepared to die?*

Go for gold!

It is important to ask ourselves: at the end of the day, what really motivates us? When all is said and done, what really matters? Because the end will determine the way we live the whole of our lives.

Gabrielle certainly knows what it is to live with the end in mind. For a good part of her life, the dream of competing in the Olympic Games absorbed her in an intensive lifestyle of training. Ranked ninth in the world in the women's 100-yard dash, she had the target, the times, and the talent.

"Competing in a sport sounds glamorous," Gabrielle continues. "But when you are standing outside ready to begin a run at five o'clock on a cold and miserable morning, with every muscle aching from a weight-training session the evening before, there is nothing to hold you there except your goals. Yet eventually, I got to a point where I realized that, as much as I loved my sport, there were some values that were even more important to me. I wanted to get married and have a family. I wanted to be more involved with my friends and in my church community. I could not fit everything into my life. This realization led me to give up my Olympic aspirations.

"My decision has not been without its difficult moments, like when the Barcelona Olympics were on. At first I could not even watch the games because it hurt too much. But during the track and field events, I read where my country's team had made the finals, so I switched on the TV to watch. There were all the familiar faces; I felt a whole mixture of emotions. Yet as I watched, I knew that I had made the right choice for me."

Your story _____

- *What values and goals motivate your life?*
- *Do you live with an end in mind?*
- *Describe a time when you significantly changed direction in your life. Why did you do this? What was the result of your action?*

38) JOHN 8:1–11
Let anyone among you who is without sin be the first to throw a stone

The ninety-day challenge

"I am trying a new tactic to help me get along with my sister," said nineteen-year-old Ann. "It is called 'the ninety-day challenge,' and I read about it in a book. It goes like this: choose a person you find hard to love. For ninety days you:

1. Speak well of that person: not a word of criticism;
2. Think only positive thoughts about the person;
3. If you are with people who are criticizing this person you must remove yourself from their company.
4. If you fail to keep your resolution—for instance, if you criticize the person—you have to start again at day one."

"So how is it going?" I asked her.

"I'm up to day twenty-seven," she replied. "It's amazing the effect this has had on me. I have started to notice all these positive qualities about my sister which I never knew she had!"

I am Abby

Our daughter, Abby, a bright and conscientious student, refused to succumb to the pressures of scholastic achievement which threatened to unbalance her perspective on life. "What I am worth is dependent on who I am as a person, not the results of an exam," was her basic philosophy. To drive the point home to herself she refused to open the envelope which arrived with the news that she had received a National Honor Society merit award.

"I want to make it in the world without my marks as a symbol of my success," she said. To this day that envelope remains unopened, framed on her wall as a symbol of her convictions: whatever my grades, I am still Abby.

Your story _____

- *Do you tend to judge people? On what basis?*
- *What criteria do you use to define yourself in relation to the world?*
- *Try the ninety-day challenge yourself.*

49

39)
They have Moses and the prophets; they should listen to them

Close call

Fighting back the tears, I slammed down the phone. My own husband…
how could he have done this to me? He knew how difficult I found raising the children, especially as he was often away on business. Yet here he was organizing a fishing trip with his friends the same week as the children were starting spring vacation!

"Is it okay with you if I go?" he had asked innocently a moment ago.

"Just fine!" I retorted through gritted teeth. What was the use of protest? He obviously did not care about me.

In my misery I began to pray, and as I did so, a clear choice emerged before me: was I going to suppress my anger and wallow in a quagmire of "poor me" self-pitying? Or would I go and confront Jack? Something inside me wanted to retreat and remain a victim. Another part of me demanded honest dialogue.

I picked up the phone. "We have to talk."

"Sure. Are you okay?"

Jack came home from work earlier that evening. We talked. We fought. We held each other. Eventually, tensions subsided. He learned something about my day-to-day stress. I learned something about his need for space and the enormous pressure he was under at work.

We both learned something about the value of talking things through, honestly and lovingly. How easily I could have remained in my self-pity for the rest of the day and probably lashed out at him that night. Efforts to reconcile are always risky, but in our marriage the benefits have been enormous.

P.S. My husband is still going fishing, but he has offered to take our two eldest sons along to give me a break. (Christine)

Your story

- *How do you typically handle situations of conflict?*
- *Describe a tough decision you have made for the sake of unity.*
- *How do you model the value of reconciliation for your family?*

40) LUKE 10:25-37
And who is my neighbor?

When you needed to hear it

My mother lives in another state so we do not see each other very often. Our phone conversations invariably end with her saying, "I love you," to which I typically reply: "Yeah, me too," in a very offhand manner.

Lately, however, I have begun to respond with: "I love you too." It probably sounds like such a little thing, but it is incredible how hard it is for me to say it. I suppose there has been a lot of damage in our relationship over the years which causes those words to stick in my throat.

It is hard to change. But I am trying. (GG)

Getting involved

Driving home through the city late one evening, I saw a man sprawled on his back at the side of the road. His body was half on the street and half on the sidewalk. Concerned but wary, I parked the car (with the engine running) and went to investigate.

The man looked to be about twenty-five years old. From the paraphernalia scattered around him, he appeared to be a drug user who had been badly beaten. For a few seconds I wrestled with my conscience. Should I risk getting involved? With all that blood around I must admit the thought of hepatitis and AIDS did cross my mind.

Being as careful as I could I took the man to hospital, all the while praying for protection. (Danny)

Your story

- *Read the Good Samaritan story from Luke's gospel (10:25-37). Retell the story using a real life setting from your own experience.*
- *What prejudices and barriers can get in the way of our showing compassion to one another?*
- *Offer a gesture of kindness to someone who is not in your social circle.*

51

6

*Stories
about Prayer*

41)
They are like angels and are children of God, being children of the resurrection

One night

The screams coming from the front of the church had a particularly tragic sound, like that of a wounded animal. On entering the church we saw a woman doubled over before the tabernacle, screaming and shouting words which at first were incoherent through her sobbing. Then we began to understand the source of her grief: "How could you let my baby die?" she kept crying.

I was somewhat shaken by the commotion, but the parish priest seemed calm and unperturbed. "It's okay, I'll stay with her," he said and sat down in a pew, patiently waiting until the woman was ready to talk.

When I saw the priest later, he was full of admiration. "Such faith, such faith," he kept saying. "That woman told God exactly what she thought of him! So many praying people hide their true selves, but this woman has brought God her real self, her deepest questions." (VC)

An image of prayer

At a parish picnic, a disgruntled three-year-old hid his face in the blanket, fiercely warding off the efforts of every well meaning adult who tried to distract him with candy and toys. This was determined sulking! Nothing was going to make this child happy. At that point the child's father came over and, without a word, enveloped the child in a strong, gentle, relentless bear hug. After initial protests, soon the child was returning the hug.

The scene spoke to me about prayer. We think we have to come to God in the right frame of mind. But God just wants to hug us, whatever our state. (Greg)

Your story _____

- *How do you pray? Why do you pray? Recall an experience of prayer where you came to God with your real self.*
- *Are you more apt to pray to God when you are happy or sad? Do you feel comfortable expressing anger to God?*

42)
When the Spirit of truth comes, he will guide you into all the truth

The fishing trip

On a recent trip to Australia, I visited the Bathurst Islands in the Timor Sea. Fishing is a long-standing tradition for this region, and the native people of the island are very protective of their fishing spots. On this particular occasion I was invited to fish for barramundi, a local catch which was quite popular among the Bathurst Islanders. My companions were a family threesome: a grandfather, his son, and his grandson.

As we made our way through the water, the grandfather was pointing out to the grandson the critical signs of nature: the shape of the clouds (that meant a storm coming); the signs on the water (that's where the fish would be); the wisdom and legends of his ancestors; and so on. Meanwhile, the father of the boy was showing the youngster how to bait the hook, cast the line, and pull in fish. The boy listened intently to his elders and enthusiastically applied himself to each task.

In this tranquil scene with father, son, and grandchild, I saw a reflection of the Trinity. To me the grandfather represents God the Father. He has the greater vision. He holds out the mythology, the symbols, and the history of the tribe. The son represents Jesus, son of God. He shows the way to grasp the vision and embody it in practice. It is the grandson who lives in the "now." The spirit of the tribe—its stories, wisdom, and traditions—must find concrete expression in the boy. For me this represents the Holy Spirit working in each of us, communicating ancient truths to each new generation.

I am grateful to this family for allowing me into their life together and enriching me with this insight. (Tom)

Your story _____

• *Tell of a time when ordinary events drew you into a greater awareness of God's presence. What did you see in physical terms? What did your inner vision see?*

• *In your own words, describe the mystery of the Trinity.*

43) JOHN 3:16–18
For God so loved the world that he gave his only Son

God's answer

Sam and Josie, a married couple in their seventies, live with the devastating effects of motorneurone disease from which Josie has suffered for the past twelve months. They are beautiful in the way they care for one another in the face of such harsh realities. Their relationship embodies the tenderness and faithfulness of divine love, a witness to all who come in contact with them. Says Sam: "When Josie's illness was first diagnosed I was praying for a miracle. I got my miracle—not in the form of her cure, but in the gift of being able to handle our circumstances with acceptance and peace."

This is my body

A mother writes: "Some of my deepest insights into the meaning of the Eucharist have come through breastfeeding. Many times, while nursing my baby, I have recalled the phrase: 'This is my body, given for you.' The same is true as well when my husband and I share an intimate moment together. There is so much I can 'say' with my body to communicate my love for Mike." (Natalie)

God's love

When our baby daughter was very sick, her ear infection made it too painful for her to lie down in her crib. My husband sat up all night cradling her feverish little body in his arms so that she and I could both sleep. This incident has given me an image of God's love which I will treasure always. (Fran)

Your story _____

- *We can make our life a prayer. Do you agree? How?*
- *In prayer, return to a time in your life when you experienced the transforming touch of God's love. Allow the memory of that experience to touch you in the present.*

44) MATTHEW 6:24–34
Strive first for the kingdom of God and his righteousness

A place of peace and prayer

A social worker who is active in parish ministry writes: my most memorable experience of prayer was with a group of teenage girls, all of whom had been through the juvenile courts for one reason or another. They lived in a small house run by the Good Shepherd sisters, an oasis of hospitality amid the day-to-day pain and danger that filled their young lives.

On Sunday nights the little community had what they called "quiet time." A statue of the Good Shepherd was placed in the center of the group. The girls would gather around and an aura of peace would descend. One of the sisters would invite "sorry" prayers, "thanking" prayers, and "asking" prayers. Everyone would pray aloud, simply, honestly, and straight from the heart.

Coming from dysfunctional homes (most had been abused in one way or another), it was not always easy for these girls to communicate appropriately in everyday life. In this prayer setting, however, they found they were able to talk and respond to the Good Shepherd in ways they could not always do with each other ("I'm sorry, Good Shepherd, for hurting Michelle when I took her jacket," "I'm sorry for stealing Cathy's boyfriend last night"). In a simple but significant way, reconciliation would occur.

Now, this is not a special incident I am describing here. The prayerfulness of this scene was repeated week after week! In my fifteen years of parish ministry I have never experienced God's peace as I have in the presence of those girls. (Chris)

Your story _____

• *Recall a memorable prayer experience in your life. Who was there? What happened? How did this experience affect your life?*
• *To what area of Christian service do you feel most called?*

45) JOHN 6:41–51
No one can come to me unless drawn by the Father who sent me

The wisdom of babes

"Look at the sky, Uncle Vince," said my six-year-old nephew. "When the clouds turn red the sun knows it's time to go down."

Overcome by a sudden desire to seize this teachable moment, I said something like, "Yes, Andrew. It is very important to take time each day to notice the beauty of nature."

This wise little kid looked up at me blankly and I realized my foolishness. What was I trying to preach to him for? Didn't he already know what I was trying to tell him? I mean, for heaven's sake, he was the one who had drawn my attention to the clouds in the first place! (VC)

"There's Jesus"

At Mass one day I saw a young couple with four squirming little children in the pew ahead. At the consecration the father lifted his littlest child into his arms. I noticed that he was pointing discreetly at the elevated host, gently whispering, "There's Jesus"—to which the child loudly yelled "What?"

Humor and all, the scene formed a precious snapshot of our faith being handed on from one generation to the next. It struck me that, regardless of whether the words made sense to the child, it was fitting she should associate that moment with the warmth of her father's embrace. (GP)

Your story

- *Who taught you to pray? How?*
- *How would you teach a child to pray?*
- *As you go through this week, allow ordinary moments to direct your thoughts and heart to God.*

46) LUKE 11:1–13
Lord, teach us to pray

Love lesson

As a youngster, my religious upbringing consisted of being packed off to Mass with the O'Brien family. While I loved the O'Briens, I somewhat resented the fact that I had to go to church while my parents did not. Beyond the resentment, there were two incidents which had a profound impact on my faith for years to come.

The first was when Mr. O'Brien suffered a stroke. I have a very strong memory of standing in the O'Briens' hallway with Mrs. O'Brien and her children, praying the rosary as we waited for the ambulance to arrive. Then, later, I remember going to the hospital to visit Mr. O'Brien for the last time. Again, I was with his family as they said the rosary at his bedside. In those moments I experienced the simple, deep faith of the O'Brien family. (MP)

Prayer time

Visiting my sister's house, I am delighted to see that her toddler is already learning to say his prayers. He's mastered the art of clasping his hands and working his way through a list of significant people in his life.

"Shall we pray for Uncle Vince?"

"Yeh," he grunts affirmatively.

"Shall we pray for grandma?"

"Yeh."

And so the litany continues.

"Now what's that special word we say to God?" coaches his mother as she seeks the "Amen" he managed yesterday.

"Please!" comes the reply. (VRC)

Your story

- *What is your earliest memory of prayer?*
- *How are you passing on the faith to the next generation?*
- *Name a prayer that means a great deal to you. Why is it so significant?*

47) JOHN 11:1–45
It is for God's glory, so that the Son of God may be glorified

Thank you

After completing a spirituality course, I wrote to the lecturer—who was also my mentor—and thanked him for the marvelous input he had given us throughout the year.

He wrote back and acknowledged my kind words saying: "Yes, it is truly a privilege to witness the wonders God is doing in our midst."

He accepted the praise, but directed it toward God. (Vic)

Always be thankful

Every day I try to thank God for the many wonderful gifts in my life. If I don't, I find myself becoming negative and intolerant of others. It is easy to be eaten up by regrets and a feeling of powerlessness over my life, particularly as I get older and find there is less and less time to pursue dreams...even worse, less inclination to do so.

When I remind myself of the great love I am given by my husband and family, of my health and the full use I have of my five senses, and of the unconditional love of God who created me and who will one day take me back to God's kingdom—then I am happy and content and thankful. But why is it so easy to take these gifts for granted, never satisfied with what I have, wanting more and more? (Jacqui)

Your story

- *Count your blessings, beginning this way: I give thanks to God for....*
- *How much is gratitude part of your daily conversation? your thoughts? your prayer life?*

48) JOHN 1:1–18

The light shines in the darkness, and the darkness did not overcome it

From a prayer journal

As I stopped to pray today, I brought to Jesus all the hopes and dreams I once held: for my marriage, my children, my parish. My faith was so strong and alive in my youth. Anything seemed possible.

And now? Well, sure, I still believe. I am just a bit disappointed. Our daughter says she has left the church. Our son seems depressed and I do not know how to help him. Our parish is bravely plugging away, but so many people just do not seem to care. I ask Jesus: what's the point of it all? I have tried so hard to be faithful to you and your people. Why do I feel like such a failure?

Quietly, in the silence of my heart, the answer came as if Jesus were speaking: it was the same for me. It was the same for those first disciples. They had the suffering, the disappointment, the confusion and sense of failure. Don't give up now. You have not lost my path. You are very much on it. Yours is a path to resurrection.

Overheard

Two young children stand before the large crucifix over the altar.
First child: What's that chocolate on his hands?
Second child: That's not chocolate, silly. That's blood!
First child: Oh! (Not sure what to make of this.)
Second child: He died, and then he came back. It was like magic!
First child: I didn't see that on TV.
Second child: That's because it's true. That's the whole story right there (pointing to the Stations of the Cross). Not in the middle (referring to the sanctuary) but there on the walls.

Your story _____

- *Have you ever felt "lifted up" by the cross? Describe what happened.*
- *What place does Jesus' death hold in your life? Where do you see it fit into the story of our salvation?*

7

Stories
of
Simplicity

49) JOHN 14:1–12
I am the way, and the truth, and the life

Blackout!

At work recently there was a sudden power failure in our building. For thirty-five minutes nothing electrical worked. "There's a blackout," I explained to a client as if it was not already obvious. "Yes, I know," she replied. "Eerie, isn't it?"

She was right. The whole atmosphere was somehow different—calmer, less pressured, quieter. The bright lights that lit up every corner of every room were gone. Instead, there was a soft glow of natural lighting from the windows, giving a new look to our surroundings.

But the silence was the most striking thing. I had never realized how much background noise existed in our offices: the hum of the computers and photocopiers, the fine buzzing sounds of the fluorescent lights, the purr of the refrigerator, the bubbling sound of the water cooler, the air conditioning—all were gone. Instead there were new sounds, people sounds.

Because it was so quiet, everyone was talking more softly but being heard more easily. I became aware of people chatting at the end of the corridor whom I would normally have never noticed. I was more aware of myself. Every movement I made produced some noise and I became very conscious of what I was doing. I felt far more in touch with my own being and with everyone around me. Then the electricity came back on. Almost instantly, we were back in a brightly lit, noisy, distracted world.

I reflected on this incident later. Life is so full of tiny distractions. which cumulatively can make us lose sight of the fundamentals of who we are and what we mean to each other. We need to take time to disconnect from things and make time for people and for God. (RP)

Your story

- *Talk about the things which keep you from being "fully alive."*
- *Do you try to schedule quiet time for yourself whenever possible? How does this affect your life-style? your faith? your relationships with others?*
- *Why is it important for people to stay connected to one another?*

50) MATTHEW 9:36—10:8
You received without payment; give without payment

Simple blessings

During my high school years, I went to a small convent school. Sr. Delores taught both English and social studies to the junior and senior class, so I came to know her well in my two last years of school. She was one of the finest teachers I ever had, bright, interesting, always ready to try new and creative ways to help us learn. Sister's work as a dedicated educator was not simply confined to the classroom. Each Saturday morning, Sr. Delores would offer tutoring for those students who wanted help in preparing for the Scholastic Achievement Tests.

I got into the college of my choice, thanks in part to Sr. Delores' help. But I found college to be far more difficult than my high school classes, and the professors less than willing to spend any time, other than class time, to help students in their studies. Realizing what a gift she had given us with her time, I wrote to Sr. Delores and thanked her for her great generosity during my high school years.

Life went on. I graduated and began a career in publishing. I forgot all about the letter, although I never forgot Sr. Dolores. Many years later, I came across her name in the obituaries of the local paper.

Her funeral was a small, quiet affair. As I watched her coffin being carried to the hearse, one of Sr. Delores' companions grabbed me by the arm. "Thank heavens you came," she said. "We have been trying to contact you." She pushed an envelope into my hand. "This is yours." Somewhat puzzled, I opened the envelope. I was looking at an aged piece of notepaper covered in adolescent scrawl—my thirty-year-old letter of thanks to Sr. Delores. "It was in her prayerbook," said the sister. "She loved your note! In her forty-six years of teaching that was her only thank-you letter." (GM)

Your story _____

- *Recall an incident where someone showed you a gesture of care that you greatly appreciated. What was said or done?*
- *Why did these words or actions mean so much to you? How did you respond?*

51) MARK 6:1–6
Prophets are not without honor, except in their hometown, and among their own kin, and in their own house

One Sunday last summer

We were having a great vacation at the beach—until Sunday came. There was no doubt we would go to Mass, but I certainly did not want to. To start, it meant getting out of a bathing suit and into "Sunday best." Then, of course, it meant going to a parish where we did not know anyone. Nor did my spirits lift upon arrival at Mass. The congregation looked like a pretty boring group. I did not know any of the songs they were singing. The boy in the pew in front was bellowing out the Mass responses, and I thought: "Can't he keep his voice down?" I mumbled the responses, withdrew into myself, and prayed quietly.

Then I happened to notice one of the altar servers singing. His face was smiling. In fact, he was enjoying the hymn so much that it was hard not to smile with him. Come to think of it, it wasn't such a bad song. The collection basket came around and a family with three little children caught my attention. The entire family was focused on the youngest as he struggled to put his coin into the basket. The whole family seemed to help each other participate. Then I took another look at the boy in front of me. He was about seven and he was looking intently at the altar, saying the responses with gusto. An uncomfortable thought crossed my mind: "What would Jesus think of my contribution to this Mass compared to these children?"

I started joining in the responses and hymns, and within minutes my attitude toward the liturgy had completely changed. I came out of church uplifted, appreciative of the opportunity to share in the faith of this beachside community, thanks to the witness of those youngsters. (Michael)

Your story _____

• *How often do you fail to recognize God's gifts in the ordinary people and opportunities which fill your life?*
• *Children (and childlike people) can be powerful prophets in our midst. Describe somebody you know who is an example of this.*

52) LUKE 4:14–21
He has anointed me to bring good news to the poor

A party with a difference

In the mail I received an invitation from a friend who was planning his fortieth birthday party. The invitation read: "I would like to celebrate my birthday with family and friends but felt that we could make it an occasion to do some good for others at the same time. So you are invited to a charity birthday party in support of Project 25.

"The aim of Project 25 is to help twenty-five families in India find a way out of poverty by helping them to get a house to live in and a means of conducting a business. So far two houses have been built and a van bought to be used in a transportation business. Please come and join us for this wonderful celebration."

Instead of coming with birthday presents, guests were asked for a donation toward Project 25. I smiled at the unusual and caring nature of the invitation. What a wonderful way for my friend to mark his fortieth year of life—by giving life to others!

Two friends

I have two friends, both people whom I love dearly. But there is a marked difference between them. When we discuss social issues like poverty and homelessness, one says, "What can we do? What simple action can we take to help this situation?" The other says, "What they (the government, the bishops) should do is...." A conversation with the first friend usually results in some action; I feel hope-filled and energized. A conversation with the second leaves me feeling despondent about the state of the world. (Anna)

Your story

• *Make a list of your resources: time, talent, and treasure. Now think of a few simple, achievable ways you can put these resources to work on an important social justice issue.*

• *Pray for people in powerful social, economic, and political positions, that they may be good stewards of the resources given them to govern.*

53) Matthew 5:1–12
Blessed are the pure in heart, for they will see God

Robbie

"Don't worry if we can't pay the rent," said Robbie. "We'll be all right as long as we stay together. We will be just as happy in a tent." Banding together with several other homeless people, Robbie had managed to rent an apartment in the downtown area of a large city. The place was attractive enough, but the rent was soaring. The small community began to search for another place to live. "We are all right so long as we can stay together," were the sacramental words which energized and supported the group. Then the phone rang. It was a friend, a parish priest from the suburbs, offering the group accommodations outside the city.

Arriving at their new address, Robbie was struck by the clarity of the stars in the pollution-free night sky. She began camping, not from necessity, but from sheer delight. The pain of rejection, abuse, institutionalization, and survival on the street was healed a bit as she lay close to the earth and watched the stars.

Robbie knew how to share her possessions. She said that she pitied rich people who kept things for themselves. "Having things you don't share only makes you miserable," she said. "God wants us to share everything. God shares the whole universe with us. If we don't share, we only have little eyes to see our own things. If we share everything, we receive the universe. It's as though we develop big eyes deep down in our hearts. Everywhere we look we can see God."

Listening to Robbie's wisdom, I ask myself: Who are the "rich" and who are the "poor" in our church? The kingdom of God is here. Those so often considered the least within society continue to tutor and lead me. (DL; *Communities Australia*, vol. 7, no. 4.)

Your story

- *What brings true happiness? Compare what is promised in the beatitudes with society's idea of happiness.*
- *How are the beatitudes lived in people around you, that is, who are the poor in spirit, the gentle, the mourners, the merciful, the peacemakers?*

54) LUKE 16:1–13
No one can serve two masters

Making waves

A group of students in the Stock Exchange? One student describes a most unlikely scene!

We found ourselves standing high on a glassed-in balcony, looking down on a huge room. We watched with fascination as a swarm of frantic, screaming human beings desperately flapped little pieces of paper and yelled into phones that seemed permanently attached to their ears. It was like looking at a unique species of animals at the zoo.

As we contemplated this scene, we began to feel depressed about society's unsatisfied hunger for money. "There's only one thing to do!" I cried. "Let's begin a wave!" (This is the motion you see at sports events, where a group stands, waves their hands over their heads from left to right, then sits down. Meanwhile, the group next to them stands and does the same; then a group next to those, and so on.)

We threw ourselves into the task. Eleven of us spread out against the glass and did the best set of waves you ever saw. We were grinning so hard it hurt our faces. The effect on the swarm was incredible. Like long grass being swept one way by a strong wind, their heads, almost as one, turned to look up at us. For a breathless second there was utter silence. Not a movement. Then it was over. Business resumed as if nothing had happened.

But for us something had changed. We were elated. We cheered and jumped around. It was a ridiculous, juvenile thing to do. Yet we felt we had achieved some tiny victory; we had made them look at us and acknowledge eleven young people who had no place in their world of material pursuit. (Jo)

Your story

• *Reflect on your use of money and material possessions. Do your actions reflect your Christian values and beliefs?*

• *How can material wealth interfere with your relationship with God and neighbor?*

55)

The child grew and became strong, filled with wisdom; and the favor of God was upon him

Bus number 398

From my seat at the rear of bus #398, I saw an elderly man struggle onto the bus. With him was a younger woman about thirty years old, obviously his daughter. Her appearance and tone of voice indicated that she had Down syndrome. The man was shaky on his feet and moved gingerly up the aisle as the bus lurched forward.

"It's okay, Dad, I'll help you," said his daughter awkwardly offering her arm as support. Her concern for him was touching.

"I'm all right, I'm all right. You be careful now," said her father, valiantly rising to the role of parental protector.

The picture of the two of them, both so vulnerable, yet a tower of strength to each other, brought tears to my eyes. It was not hard to imagine the struggles life had set before them. I thought of the father as a younger man; the mixture of joy and pain at his child's birth, his effort to care for her throughout her life, and now, in his later years, having to face the fact that one day she would be left to fend for herself. I imagined the daughter's fear. How hard for anyone to lose a parent let alone for someone with the mind of a child.

By the time I got off the bus my whole perception of life had changed. How blessed I am, I thought. I have health, family, friends, security. What a responsibility I have to live up to my potential. How often I take it all for granted. It has taken the loving witness of this man and his daughter—both "poor" in the eyes of the world—to reveal to me life's real riches. (Michael)

Your story

- *What is really important in life? Name some of your deepest values.*
- *Why is it easy to lose sight of these values?*
- *Who or what helps you to keep focused on your priorities?*

56) Matthew 1:18–24
They shall name him Emmanuel, "God is with us"

God is near

As I look out my office window I have a view of a small park. This morning I noticed an elderly couple walking through this park. The man was blind and his wife guided him as they walked. "How sad that he cannot see all those magnificent trees," I thought to myself. At that very moment, the blind man stopped by a large tree. He ran his hand up and down the bark and seemed to delight in the texture under his palm.

Later, during my lunch hour, I walked over to that same tree and felt for the first time the intricate lines and furrows of its bark. Funny how I had walked through this park for ten years and never before stopped to notice this detail of natural beauty. It took a blind man to open my eyes. (Lee)

Plain and simple

Bill and Cheryl are an ordinary middle-aged couple. He's balding. She's slightly overweight. They have never won any awards or earned a lot of money. But after thirty-five years of marriage, they are still together. They have raised five kids. They are faithful to their parish. They organize the local Boy Scout troop. They look out for their neighbors. They have a "no frills" goodness which is so precious in today's turbulent world.

People relate to them as a unit. If you meet Bill down the street, he'll mention Cheryl in the next sentence. It's the same with her. They have a natural openness and interest in others. People just enjoy being around them. There is undoubtedly something very attractive about this couple. It's not their status, money, or achievements. What they have is love. (Steve)

Your story _____

• *Name some of the ways we can shut both God and the people we love out of our lives, e.g., through our preoccupation with TV, outside activities, or negative thoughts.*

8

Stories
of
Community

57)
MATTHEW 13:44–52
Every scribe…is like the master of a household who brings out of his treasure what is new and what is old

Mrs. Lawrence

I have always been a fairly outgoing sort of person. At three years of age I wandered into the house next door, parked myself on a kitchen stool, and introduced myself to Mrs. Lawrence, our surprised neighbor!

Mrs. Lawrence was a widow whose husband had died of cancer after one year of marriage. She took an instant liking to me, and for the next thirteen years I would visit her every day. Sitting on that same kitchen stool, we would have marvelous chats. Even today I can still picture that kitchen, its unusual ornaments on the shelf: seashells inscribed with Bible stories in tiny writing. It was Mrs. Lawrence who taught me how to cook, sew, crochet, and argue. I recall, too, her enormous "magical" garden where I lived many a childhood fantasy. She was always there for me, unconditionally.

And so it was until I turned fifteen, when Mrs. Lawrence had to have an "ear operation." I found out later that this was adult-speak for "breast cancer." Mrs. Lawrence never returned from hospital, and I lost a great friend without ever saying goodbye. I had hoped to be able to keep sitting on that kitchen stool for many more years, but it was not to be.

It wasn't until I was well into my thirties that my mother brought out some of things Mrs. Lawrence had left her. I couldn't believe my eyes! Among them were the seashells with tiny writing that had been part of the kitchen scene so familiar to my memory. The sight of the shells brought me back many years, when I was once again sitting in the kitchen, sharing stories in an atmosphere of love. (MG)

Your story

- *What sort of atmosphere does your home have? When a visitor walks in, can he or she sense that this is a loving, faith-filled place?*
- *In the gospel cited above, the kingdom of God is described as a treasure hidden in a field. What treasures are hidden in your life? How can you bring them out to share with others?*

58) Luke 14:1, 7–14

For all who exalt themselves will be humbled, and those who humble themselves will be exalted

Humbled and exalted

A priest—we'll call him Fr. Frank—was visiting a L'Arche community in Europe. (L'Arche communities are homes for mentally and physically disabled adults who live together and support one another.) Fr. Frank was not a well man. He was recovering from a nervous breakdown and, although feeling stronger, had not yet regained full health.

On this particular day, the priest who was scheduled to celebrate Mass with the community did not show up. Fr. Frank offered to help. The people gratefully accepted and together they began to pray the Mass. But within a short time Fr. Frank became very nervous and lost all confidence. He stumbled and mumbled his way to the end of Mass, feeling devastated and humiliated. How upset he was to have let the community down in this simple task! He wanted to run away and hide from the people who saw him in his weakness and helplessness.

After Mass the people came forward and hugged him. They were smiling and crying at the same time. They were saying to him that this was one of the most beautiful Masses they had ever been to! Fr. Frank could not understand their exuberant joy, as he was feeling the opposite. Resisting their praise, he asked, "How can you possibly describe this Mass as you have?" They replied, "But Father, you are just like us. Thank you!" These people, so often rejected by society, had recognized something of themselves in this priest as he celebrated the Eucharist. He truly represented Christ among them.

Your story _____

• *Think of a recent social gathering you attended. Who was there? Who was not? What social code was at work? How might Jesus have responded to the situation?*

• *How do you feel about humility? Do you see it as a sign of weakness, or as a sign of strength? Why?*

59)

Let your light shine before others, so that they may see your good works and give glory to your Father in heaven

Mrs. Chu

When I was eighteen I lived in the inner city. At one end of the street there stood a church and at the other end of the street was a takeout hamburger place run by a Chinese lady, Mrs. Chu. To my youthful way of thinking, these two places represented opposite approaches to faith. Unfortunately, this particular church appeared to be an unfriendly institution as it was usually locked up except for its two Masses on Sunday. Mrs. Chu's eatery, on the other hand, was a revelation to the locals.

You could not be anonymous around Mrs. Chu. Upon entering her shop she cried out "Hello there!" followed by the most personal question she could muster in front of the waiting patrons. You see, Mrs. Chu knew the whole street and, through Mrs. Chu, the inhabitants of the street knew the whole street. So, while waiting for your hamburger, you would find out that Mr. So-and-So at Number 29 had just had an operation, and Mrs. So-and-So at Number 25 was expecting a new baby.

There was such a down-to-earth trustworthiness about Mrs. Chu that you really didn't mind telling her things. Her manner was always in good humor. She never seemed to dislike anyone. Over the two years that I lived there I saw Mrs. Chu involved in something that was much more than making hamburgers. If someone had a problem, Mrs. Chu had a reassuring word. If someone was down, Mrs. Chu would pick them up. By night, I knew she helped out at a soup kitchen for the city's needy.

I think people went to Mrs. Chu's for the experience—to share a bit of community and to take away a bit of her vitality and goodness. I am sure this was true because, to be perfectly honest, she made a terrible hamburger! (Mark)

Your story

- *God wants true holiness, not piety. What does this mean to you?*
- *Think about some practical ways of enlivening your faith, e.g., join a faith sharing group, sign up for a retreat, pray for conversion, or get involved in a mission.*

60)

Kindness of strangers

On Tuesday I received a very distraught phone call from my fifteen-year-old daughter who had found herself stranded at the train station in a small country town. She was on her way home to Canberra only to find that her bus connection had been cancelled. There was no easy way for her to get back home from that location, nor did she have much money with her. At a distance of 200 miles, this was the stuff of a mother's nightmare. I knew of no one in this town whom I could call to "rescue" my daughter and ensure her safety while I made the three-hour car trip to pick her up.

The hand of providence, however, was guiding our movements. I decided to call the Catholic church in this town to seek assistance. The two women who received my call, the parish secretary and one of the nuns from the parish team, immediately allayed my fears. Within fifteen minutes, Sister Ellen made the trip to the station, collected my daughter and took care of her until I arrived later in the afternoon. I knew neither of these women and had never spoken to them until my phone call, yet I felt secure and confident that I could rely on them as I could on anyone in my own parish.

There is some intangible bond and unspoken allegiance between people of my generation in the church. This bond is not dependent on a personal knowledge of the other nor is it restricted by distance. I was drawing on the power of a shared past and pilgrimage which provide me with an understanding of belonging. (Therese; first published in *Australian Catholics*, Autumn 1996)

Your story _____

- *How do you feel about the people in your parish? Do you trust them to help you if necessary? Does this feeling extend to other parishes, as well?*
- *What makes for a Christian community? Is it any different than the community spirit offered by a social club or other organization? Why or why not?*

61) MARK 12:38–44
This poor widow has put in more than all those who are contributing to the treasury

Musings of a small country churchgoer

I went to Mass recently at a busy city cathedral, and am still suffering from culture shock. The contrast with our little country church was startling. The men in the congregation all wore suits. We don't see suits at our church except at an occasional wedding or funeral: "jumpers and jeans" is more the rule.

The floral arrangements at the cathedral were magnificent professional sculptures with gold-painted foliage. The flowers at our church are from our gardens, lovingly, though somewhat inexpertly, arranged. The magnificent pipe organ filled the huge cathedral with majestic and triumphal sound. The young cantor ably led the singing—well, really, it was almost a solo performance. Our church music is accompanied by a $300 keyboard, four college students on guitars, and four other students on recorders. They start up the singing and the congregation joins in.

It must be hard to get a feeling of community in a cathedral. If I was sick or grieving in a cathedral parish, would anyone know? Back home in our parish, someone would bring a cake, casserole, or just lend a friendly ear.

I once thought it would be great to live in a big parish with access to liturgy and musical expertise. But after Mass at the city cathedral I am very content with what we have back home. And I know God must look down on the cathedral and our little church and not see the difference. To God it must be his people praising him in the way they know best. (Glenys)

Your story

- *In what church setting are you most comfortable?*
- *Is the atmosphere and assembly of a parish important to you, or is the liturgy all that matters?*
- *Think of an act of generosity on your part in recent days. Did you give from your excess funds or from your necessary funds?*

62) LUKE 10:1–12,17–20
Ask the Lord to send out laborers into his harvest

A parish with a mission

I will never forget the time I broke my left foot; it happened the week after my wife, Angela, came home from hospital with our sixth child. While I was out of work recuperating, things were pretty tough on Angela. But it got much worse! Two weeks after I returned to work, Angela broke her foot. This was a real disaster because I had used up all my sick time and there was no way I could afford to take more time off work. How on earth were we going to cope with running a household with six children, the youngest a newborn?

At this point, I contacted the pastoral care coordinator in our parish. Almost the next day she appeared with a list of parishioners who were willing to help us out. Each night, someone came by with a prepared dinner for all of us. During the day, various women came by for a few hours to help watch the children and do some of the household chores. Everyone was friendly and anxious to please. My wife and I were astounded, and overwhelmed with gratitude.

Apart from being a godsend to us, this was also an opportunity to meet some of the parishioners in a different light. Not just in passing at church, but in a more neighborly setting. My wife and I can't wait for the opportunity to repay the kindness! (LR)

Words of life

Sam and Lynn just told me they are expecting their fifth child. "That's fantastic!" I said. "Let me babysit the other children so you two can have a night out to celebrate!" Lyn was both grateful and surprised. "You are the first person who has responded positively. Most people say we are crazy!" (RC)

Your story _____

- *What do you see as your Christian mission? How do you carry this out?*
- *Pray for vocations, not only for the priesthood and religious life, but also for the various Christian ministries.*

63) LUKE 7:36—8:3
Your faith has saved you; go in peace

The Christmas spirit

Annette, a single mother with four young children in tow, stood wearily at the bus stop. It had been a long day. The stores and traffic were frantic. The Christmas pageant they had attended earlier should have left her in better spirits, but here she was feeling rundown and lonely. "God, please get me home without a nervous breakdown," she prayed.

After what seemed like eternity, the bus came and Annette struggled up to the driver, balancing bags and children while she fished out her fare card. "All I want to do is sit down," she thought as she blinked back tears of fatigue and moved gingerly down the aisle.

"Just a minute, Ma'am," the bus driver called out to her. Annette returned to the front of the bus where the driver closely inspected her fare card. "OK, thank you." The bus driver seemed satisfied and the trip home continued uneventfully. She didn't give the incident another thought.

The day before Christmas, the doorbell rang. There stood the bus driver and his wife, laden with groceries and gifts. "I thought you looked a bit downcast the other day," the bus driver said. "I hope you don't mind, but I noted your address on your fare card. Would you and your family like to join us for Christmas dinner?"

Your story _____

- *How can you tell when someone is hurting inside even without them saying anything?*
- *How can you reach out to a hurting person in the coming week?*
- *Has someone ever been a healing presence to you?*

64)

One Sunday

I had just sat down at Mass one Sunday when I became aware of a terrible smell coming from a disheveled looking gentleman sitting in a nearby seat. The stench was so bad that it did not take long before four rows of people behind the man had cleared out! I too began to gag on the odor. Fortunately, I found that if I turned my head in a particular position I could catch a slight breeze through the window which alleviated the discomfort.

I really felt for this man and wondered about his situation. When I turned to him at the sign of peace, I made a point of looking him in the eye and offering him a sincere handshake. The man had his head down—he looked kind of ashamed—and it was a second or two before he cautiously looked at me and returned my handshake.

In that moment I felt the depth of his sadness and isolation, and wondered how long it had been since this man had felt the physical touch of another human being. Returning from communion, I saw that the man had left the church. I ran outside after him. I guess I just wanted to ask him, "Are you all right?" perhaps ask him his name. But he had gone. (Leon)

Your story

• *Reflect on this story. Would you have been one of the people who moved away? or would you have stayed and offered a handshake?*

• *What are your needs: spiritual, physical, and emotional? How are they met?*

81

9

*Stories
of Justice*

65) LUKE 12:13–21
Be on your guard against all kinds of greed; for one's life does not consist in the abundance of possessions

Life is short; be generous

"Life is short," said the student next to me. "You've got to make the most of it, now. If you want a car, you go out and get that car! If you want to go on vacation, you make sure you go on that vacation!"

"Yeah, that's right." Affirmative grunts resonated all around the room. "I mean, we've got to get ahead now, while we're young!" said another student. "As soon as I graduate I'm going to work in Europe for a couple of years. Then I'll take some time off and just travel around." The rest of the students nodded in agreement. "Mmm....yeah...great idea."

We were fifteen occupational therapy students in a special tutorial. The topic was "attitudes in life and death." And this was where the day's discussion had taken us, into a selfish spiral of "give me, get me, I deserve it." My stomach felt queasy.

"Um...I don't mean to be a downer or anything," I began. "But everything we have been talking about is what we want. Don't you think we should be thinking about how our skills might be used, say, for people in poorer countries?"

The tutor responded, "Yes, but don't forget, Trish, that wherever you work, you'll always be helping people in some way. It's the nature of the profession."

"Yes, I know, but...."

The discussion took off again. I felt like my comments had not really been heard, but later a student came up to me and said, "I was thinking the same thing but I was too shy to speak up." I wish she had. (Tricia)

Your story

• *Consider the riches you bring to your local community, e.g., knowledge, income, time, possessions. How are they used for the benefit of others?*
• *How are your gifts used to spread the message of the gospel?*

66) JOHN 18:33–37
Everyone who belongs to the truth listens to my voice

The true path of faith

The headline flashed across the world hours after her death: "Aussie nun executed after terrorist sham trial." Irene McCormack was a Josephite sister from Perth, Australia, who dedicated her life to relief work among the village people of Huasahuasi, Peru. Her pride and joy was the simple schoolroom and library which she had set up for the benefit of the children. While aware of the threats of the fanatical terrorist group *Sendero Luminoso* (Shining Path), Irene chose to remain in Huasahuasi in solidarity with the people and as a Christian witness.

On this particular evening, May 21, 1991, about sixty terrorists converged upon the village. After sabotaging the village energy supply they rounded up Irene and four village officials. The victims were then subjected to a sham trial in the village square. "Here we have five people who have been cheating the people," began the terrorist leader. He likened Irene to a channel for dirty water which was contaminating the country with deteriorating American merchandise.

The people protested, saying she was an Australian, not an American, and that she was dedicated to working with children. But the terrorist leader retorted, "If there are lawyers here, let them come up and die with her!" Then the terrorists charged their arms and shot Irene and the four men in the head. There was panic among the people. Some fainted. Some wept. Others cried out. Others ran. (From the *Catholic Mission*, 1995)

Your story _____

• *Irene McCormack was one of many contemporary missionaries who place their lives at risk for the sake of gospel values. What impact does her story have on you?*
• *Would you be prepared to die for your beliefs?*
• *Name some of the hardships and challenges faced by missionaries.*

67) JOHN 10:11–18
I lay down my life in order to take it up again

A respectful response

Barbara was taking two elderly neighbors on an outing. They loved the river, and the two-hour cruise offered a relatively inexpensive way to enjoy a Sunday morning. As they approached the ticket booth, the two senior citizens pulled out their senior citizen cards and were handed children's tickets.

"Oh, excuse me, Miss," said one. "You've given us children's tickets."

"That's right. Half price. Seniors get a child's ticket," came the I've-said-this-for-the-fiftieth-time-today reply.

"Oh, I see."

The two senior women shared an embarrassed chuckle as they took their tickets and moved on. The incident was brief but the sting of humiliation lingered and did not escape the sensitivities of their friend Barbara. The next day she paid a visit to the cruise office and related the incident to the manager.

"So I wonder if there is some way you could distinguish between the tickets. Even just a stamp on the adult ticket. It's just a small thing, but I think our older folk deserve the respect." The manager was surprised but received her words with empathy. Yes, he saw her point. It was an unfortunate oversight...he would attend to it.

Within a week procedures at the cruise ticket booth had changed.

Your story

• *Recall a time when you felt valued as a unique, human person. How did it feel?*

• *"Respect for human dignity" is an often-quoted phrase. What does it mean to you? Discuss examples of what this phrase means in practice.*

Fighting for justice

I will always remember the parish catechist I met when, as a young seminarian, I visited an isolated part of the Philippines. Under the circumstances, she had everything to lose. She lived in a climate of political conflict and social unrest. She trained Christian leaders in the many small *barrios* away from the main parishes. To put it bluntly, her life was in danger. Yet she possessed no gun to defend herself. She was a grandmother who might have preferred nothing more than to spend her twilight years surrounded by her family.

I expected to hear her speak to me about theories, theologies, and social justice. But as we traveled to her barrio, her conversation was entirely about people and their lives. She asked many questions about my own family. I can recall only one thing that whole day which could be called advice. She told me that when I became a priest I should always "remember to let people help you. The people will want to help you, Tony." She was a remarkably generous and wise woman.

This woman's Christian life taught me that loving one's enemies is largely about holding an abiding hope in people in times of trouble and conflict. It is not as simplistic as letting people say or do what they like to you. It is a hope reliant on the action of the Spirit; never giving up while there is something to give. I hope I will always remember her witness. (Tony)

Your story _____

• *Think of a situation of injustice which angers you. Are you tempted to respond to this situation with "violence," that is, destructive words or behavior?*

• *What constructive, love-driven response can you make when you are confronted with injustice?*

69)

Colette

As my friend, Colette, and I traveled home from school one afternoon, we came across one of the city's homeless men doubled up over the main steps of the entrance to the train station. With one filthy hand gripped around a wine bottle, the man's humped shape made an unwelcome obstacle for the rush-hour crowds that streamed around and over him. To my surprise, Colette stopped, bent down and covered the man's filthy hand with hers.

"Are you all right?" she asked gently. The man, who up to now had seemed unconscious, slowly stirred and seemed to be trying to say something. Eventually he scratched some letters in the dust: MONEY.

At that point a policeman came by. "What's going on here?"

"I think this man is hungry," said Colette. "But if I give him money he will probably spend it on alcohol."

"There's a shelter down the road that can help this guy," said the policeman. "I'll give them a call."

While we waited for help to arrive, Colette bought the man a cup of coffee and a sandwich. "I can't believe all those people just walked right past him like that," she said incredulously.

"Incredible," I agreed, although not without an edge of guilt. Had I not been with Colette, I too would probably have walked past the man. She taught me a lot that day about practicalities of Christian love. (Jenny)

Your story _____

- *Describe a time when you were challenged to live up to your own principles of justice. What happened?*
- *Did you come away changed by this experience? In what way?*

70) Mark 7:31–37
And immediately his ears were opened, his tongue was released, and he spoke plainly

Point taken

One afternoon a group of young people on vacation together turned on the television to amuse themselves. On the screen was an American television personality fielding the questions and comments of an opinionated studio audience. The point of discussion? A fourteen-year-old boy was marrying a forty-year-old woman. The unusual couple sat at the front of the studio and the live discussion raged around them. Among the young people, as well, a fiery debate about youth, sex, and marriage began to gather momentum. This was juicy stuff!

One person, however, responded differently. "I hate seeing people's personal lives exploited like that," said Scott. "I'm going for a walk." And with that he left the room. The conversation continued, but with a little less steam. Two more people left the room. A short while later the television was switched off.

Scott's reaction taught us a lesson. Not because he moralized, but simply because he showed respect for the dignity of two strangers who had their own lives to live. (GP)

Decisions

Last year, Tom was offered a job for double the salary of his present teaching position. It was an attractive offer. Yet, after talking it through with his family, he turned it down. His wife explains their decision: "Tom is a father figure at school. Many kids confide in him about their personal hassles. We estimate he saves at least one teenager from suicide and one baby from being aborted each year. Even if they pay him double the salary at a new job, it's just not worth it."

Your story _____

• *What is your reaction to exploitation when you encounter it on television or in magazines and newspapers?*
• *Think of a situation where you can easily take people for granted. How can you change your behavior in this regard?*

71) LUKE 13:1–9
Unless you repent, you will all perish as they did

The poor box

In church one day, my two-year-old son entertained the congregation with a new little game. Taking a dime from my purse, he toddled over to the poor box, pushed the money through the slot and came back for another dime. The trips to the poor box continued.

Well, that was well and good. But then, on his fifth trip, he grabbed a twenty-dollar bill from my purse and headed for the poor box! Quiet gasps came from the pews around me. Whoops! Enough of that game. Instinctively, I intercepted my son and distracted him from his fascination with the poor box.

Later, as I reflected on this incident, I was filled with a sense of shame. My child had challenged my middle-class parameters of generosity. Why not put twenty dollars in the poor box? Perhaps I am more attached to my money than I would like to think. (Therese)

Cheap jeans

A social worker recalls his middle-class assumptions being inadvertently challenged by this conversation with a homeless woman. "Sandy," I said, "do you know where I can buy a pair of cheap jeans?"

"Well, you can go to the Salvation Army store and get a pair for about $10.00, or just opposite the Town Hall there's a Woolworths where you can get a pair for around $25."

"Thanks," I said, mentally storing the information. Then I noticed her giving me a strange look. It was a look of genuine puzzlement. "You've already got jeans," she said, pointing to my faded denim-clad legs. "Why would you want another pair?" (DP)

Your story _____

- *How does your use of material goods contribute to the well-being of others?*
- *How do your financial decisions help—or hinder—other people?*
- *What are you teaching others about generosity and justice?*

72)
Whoever does not take up the cross and follow me is not worthy of me

The rebel

It is amazing the insights that can come to you as you get older. Looking back, I realize that for years our family operated with an unwritten rule, which we all abided by. We were a "happy" family; no problems, no maladjustments. Oh, of course there were tensions as in every normal family. But we never fought. We just withdrew: cold silence, avoidance of eye contact, absence of affection. No one shared what they really felt. But no one ever fought. No one, that is, until our youngest turned fifteen.

She reacted to tension differently. She yelled. She stamped her foot and used bad language. She slammed doors and told us where to go. In a word, she fought. And of course, she was the one perceived as the "problem child." We ended up having family counseling; anything to help her and her problem. She was the one who had disturbed the family status quo. She was the impossible one, the black sheep who would not fit in.

We struggled through those years. We survived, with scars to show. But it was not until years later that I saw my daughter in a new light. I saw that she had in fact been challenging an unhealthy family myth. She was the only one who had the courage and inclination to do so. She brought things out in the open; demanded that we confront each other rather than sweep things under the carpet; rejected the "cold war" option. Her "problem" was, in fact, us and our unwritten law: we don't fight. In our family, anger and hurt were submerged, suppressed under chilling withdrawal. But no one ever fought. Except our youngest child.

Your story

- *How does your family handle internal tensions and conflict? How do you feel about this?*
- *Sometimes "keeping the peace" can be a way of avoiding or confronting the truth. What are some healthy ways to deal with disagreement in your family? with friends? with coworkers?*

10

*Stories
about Not
Giving Up*

Star struck!

When I first met Michael I did not even notice his wheelchair. I was just mesmerized by the vitality of his presence. I had never met such a good-looking twenty-four year old who played such a mean guitar, and who seemed to love God and people in such an open and disarming manner. The fact that he was a paraplegic from a motorcycle accident was completely irrelevant to me. I was fourteen years old and star struck!

Michael was my guitar teacher. I loved those lessons because we would usually end up talking about life, relationships, and God. With Michael you could not talk about anything without bringing God into the conversation somehow. (The very first chords he taught me were for the hymn "Go Tell It on the Mountain.") His friendship and Christian witness opened up for me a whole new awareness of Jesus.

As I grew older and came to know Michael better, I was amazed to realize that he often suffered from depression. In view of the enthusiasm he exuded to others you would never have known that he went through some deep spiritual struggles.

We lost contact for many years. When I heard of him again he had married and adopted a foster child, a victim of child abuse who suffered severe behavioral problems. After a couple of years of loving struggle he and his wife adopted a second child, also a victim of child abuse.

That was typical of Michael. He had an enormous love that shone through even in the darkest of situations. To this day, I regard him as my "star of Bethlehem" who led me to Christ. (Lee)

Your story _____

• *Recall someone who has been a beacon of light to you. What was it that made them special?*

• *Christ is light to the world. What does this phrase mean in a practical way? How can you live it out in your daily life?*

74) MARK 1:29–39
He cast out many demons

Sam

Our third son, Sam, was the easiest baby—happy, secure, contented. In grammar school he was the angel in the nativity play for two years running. "A beautiful child, a priest for sure," according to the dear Sisters who taught him. In high school, however, Sam underwent a transformation. Whatever the reasons (and we still ask ourselves "why?") he began to be in trouble at school and with the police. Court cases and fines followed. I can still recall the shame of waiting outside the local courtroom in the company of people I would not have considered my company. (I do now!)

How did we cope with all this? All we could do was let him know that we still loved him, although we did not like what he was doing. We also prayed a lot, begging God to let Sam find his way through all this without permanent damage.

Well, he's getting there. The turning point came when we received this letter:

Dear Mom and Dad,

I am writing this letter because I have probably never told you how much I appreciate you. I am very grateful to have had wonderful, caring parents. I am sure that if I had not, I would be in a lot more trouble than I am.

I know I have caused you some hassles and sleepless nights, and I am sorry. I think I am a lot more stable now. I am trying to get my life together so that you can be proud of me. Mom and Dad, I love you and I am grateful, even though it doesn't always show.

Love, Sam

(Courtesy, *Catholic Ethos* (no. 12), National Catholic Education Commission)

Your story _____

- *How would you respond to your child if his or her life turned bad?*

75) LUKE 18:1–8
Because this widow keeps bothering me, I will grant her justice

Safia's story

When Safia was nine months pregnant, the police came to her home in the middle of the night and dragged her away to prison. (This happened in Somalia in 1985.) Safia was put into a dark, damp prison cell where, three days later, she gave birth to a son. The security forces took the baby away from her and sent Safia back to her cell.

Safia had not committed any crime. In fact, it is still not clear why she was arrested except that she had criticized the authorities and belonged to the "wrong" ethnic group. Safia was tortured in the early days of her imprisonment. After ten months, a mock trial was held and she was sentenced to life imprisonment with no recourse to appeal.

By this time Amnesty International had learned of Safia's plight. After confirming the fact that she was unjustly held as a prisoner of conscience, Amnesty launched three campaigns requesting her release. Volunteers wrote hundreds of letters and postcards to the Somalian government. They sent telegrams. They publicized the story in their local newspapers and on radio and television. They raised money to help pay for more appeals on Safia's behalf.

Meanwhile, the torture had stopped but prison conditions remained harsh. Safia became very ill but was given no medical care. Amnesty again went to work. Soon the Somali Minister of Health had received countless messages of concern from all parts of the world. Within a month, Safia had received medical treatment. Another year passed and Safia was still in prison. Amnesty volunteers continued to demand her freedom. At last, four years after her imprisonment, Safia was set free. She was reunited with her family. They settled in England and began the process of putting their life back together again. (Courtesy of Amnesty International, 1992)

Your story _____

- *Is there an area of your life where you have given up? Why? What will it take to try again?*
- *Where do you find hope in times of darkness?*

76) MATTHEW 25:14–30
You have been trustworthy in a few things, I will put you in charge of many things

Nina's story

I looked out at the sea of faces, all enrolled in a parish ministry course, and there was Nina. Nina's face, normally so bright and vivacious, told a story of grief. Her baby had died; it was her second miscarriage. A beautiful chapter of life had turned into a nightmare, and Nina was living it, even now, as the group talked about the power of our dreams to make a difference to the mission of the church. My heart sank. Where are Nina's dreams now? I thought. How can we speak of power and hope when this woman is facing such debilitating pain?

Yet the Spirit touched Nina in her grief. Within ten weeks she had created a ministry of healing for her own fellow parishioners. Her plan had been simple and straightforward, drawing upon the loving support of her husband and empowered by that rare depth of insight that comes through suffering.

She had gathered some women in the parish who, known to only a few, had also endured a miscarriage. They came together to share one another's silent grief, to pray together and to receive some practical input from a trained counselor whom Nina had contacted through a local church agency.

Nina taught us all something very special about putting our lives at the service of God's kingdom, no matter how impoverished we may feel. With what she had, Nina gave.

Your story

- *If you are experiencing loss and grief: is there some way God wants to use your experience to bring life to others?*
- *If your life is going well, how can you give a little bit more of your time, treasure, and talents to ease somebody else's pain?*

77) JOHN 15:1–8
If you abide in me, and my words abide in you, ask for whatever you wish, and it will be done for you

The wisdom of Mrs. Jamison

"I pray every day for perseverance in the faith," said my elderly neighbor, Mrs. Jamison. At the time I was puzzled. Why would such a lovely woman, who had been devoted to her family and her Catholic faith all her life, a daily communicant and a member of the Rosary Society who still gave money to the missions, be worried about losing her faith?! Surely at age ninety, with a track record like that you can start to take some things for granted.

It was not until ten years later, with a bit more life experience under my belt, that I began to fathom the wisdom of this holy woman. In the zeal of my youth I never doubted that my faith would carry me through for life. I was committed and prepared to renew that commitment every day. Or so I thought.

With the passage of time and the strain of life's trials, I am much more conscious now of my own vulnerability. The key to faith is not my own efforts but God's grace. It is not self-reliant strength but my utter dependence on God that will keep me faithful to the end. Which is why—whether I am nineteen or ninety—I will never cease praying for the gift of faith. (Anna)

Your story _____

• *What does it mean to stay connected to Jesus, the vine? How can you do this? How do you stay "connected" to your loved ones who have died?*
• *What are some of the relationships which are channels of grace in your life? What do you think makes them so?*

98

78)
Into your hands I commend my spirit

I will survive!

In a two-week period, my whole life was uprooted. Within just fourteen days my impending marriage was off, I had changed jobs, and moved to a new town. While life went on externally, my insides were doing somersaults. I found myself crying on the bus on the way to work, acting happy and enthusiastic at work, then crying on the bus all the way home. Each evening I would go to sleep despairing of ever feeling normal again.

During this difficult time, I cherished the support of two friends who had been through similar trying times. They were empathetic and reassuring: "You will get through this. You can survive. God will not give you anything that you cannot handle."

They were right. Today, from a much happier standpoint in life, I am grateful to be able to offer similar reassurance to others who feel their world is falling apart. Yes, it is okay. You will survive. Trust that God will bring you through. (CP)

The first step

We have this great guy in our parish choir. He is in his sixties, has the most beautiful smile, and is just so affirming of people. He strikes you as being a conservative, well-dressed, professional man, so you can imagine my surprise when I heard him tell his story.

For years he was an alcoholic who had given up on life and lived on the streets. The thing that turned his life around was that he was befriended by a stray dog and began to care for it. It soon became obvious to him that when he was drunk he could not care for the dog. That was the beginning of his upward spiral. (GJ)

Your story _____

• *Recall a difficult time in your life. Who or what got you through that time? Where did God fit in that picture?*
• *What would you say to someone who is going through a difficult time?*

79) MARK 4:35–44
Why are you afraid? Have you still no faith?

Two photos

Vietnam, 1972. A nine-year-old Vietnamese girl is running naked along a war-torn road, screaming in anguish as napalm sears her body. This photograph is all too familiar to many of us.

The photo was especially poignant for me. The first time I had laid eyes on it I, too, was a nine-year-old girl. Twenty-four years ago, the image of my peer had made a deep impression on my young mind, filling me with sadness and a sense of the futility and destruction of war.

I had always assumed the child in the photo had died in the war. But today I am looking at that photo again. It accompanies an article which also shows a second photograph, that of a smiling thirty-three-year-old Vietnamese woman. The child, Kim Phuc, survived the war and now, after years of physical and emotional recovery, lives in Canada with her husband and two-year-old son. In a dramatic public gesture of forgiveness and reconciliation, Kim recently traveled to Washington to lay a wreath at the Vietnam Veterans' Memorial. She addressed a crowd of several thousand people and spoke words of forgiveness, peace, and her faith in God who "saved my life and gave me faith and hope."

"Even if I could talk face-to-face with the pilot who dropped the bombs, I would tell him: 'We cannot change history, but we should try to do good things for the present and the future to promote peace,'" Kim Phuc was reported as saying.

I looked at the two photos for a long time: the terrified nine-year-old and the smiling thirty-three-year-old mother. An image of anguish and an image of peace; a startling contrast and reminder that God's loving presence abides with us always, even through the most grievous chapters of human history. (Anna)

Your story

- *How does your faith help you deal with the atrocities of the world?*
- *Have you ever been the victim of grave injustice? What was the outcome? Who, if anyone, helped you through it?*

80) JOHN 6:51–58
The bread that I will give for the life of the world is my flesh

Connections

My colleague, Tim, was a Catholic who had left the church many years ago. He had been hurt by some of the religious who taught him as well as by some of the parishioners who had let his family down in their hour of need. As a result he no longer went to church and refused to send his children to a Catholic school.

He knew I was involved in my parish and we often talked about our Catholic connection—or as much as you could in ten minutes at coffee break in a crowded lunch room. I would listen to his story and opinions. He was a good, caring man with strong principles and many gifts. I could not help thinking remorsefully that his bad experiences as a Catholic were not only unfortunate for him, but for the church. How we could use a man like that in my own parish!

As much as I empathized with him, I was not prepared to let him off the hook that easily. Tim was a guy who could handle a bit of a challenge. So I would also say things to him like: "It's no good staying outside and complaining about things...come in and help us make a difference," and "The church is like a family. Sure, people let you down but they never stop being family to you."

Tim left work to begin a new career as an accountant. I called soon after he left to see how he was doing. The first week had been a disaster, and he asked me to pray for him. At first I thought he was joking. But then I realized this was not a joke but a serious request. Perhaps those chats during coffee break had touched a chord after all. (CL)

Your story _____

- *Think of some objections people have to God and to the church. Then ask yourself these questions: Why do I believe? How have I come to that belief? How do I work at strengthening my faith?*
- *Do you know someone who has left the church in anger? How do you respond to him or her?*

11

Stories
of Witness

81) MATTHEW 21:33–43
The kingdom of God will be taken away from you and given to a people that produces the fruits of the kingdom

One of the band

Saturday night. I was loading the gear for our band into a nightclub in a pretty rough part of town when a small group of boys—about thirteen years old—crowded around me and began firing off questions.

"You in the band, man?"

"No, man, I just carry the gear."

"Are you on smack (heroin)?"

"No. Just because you're with a band doesn't mean you're on drugs."

"What bands do you like?'

"Oh, the Stones mainly...and a few others."

"Do you like Nirvana?"

"They're a bit heavy for me. Do you like them?"

"Yeah."

"What songs of theirs do you like?"

"I don't know any."

(Laughing). "But you know you like them!"

"Yeah...Nirvana was on smack."

And so the conversation continued. Later, it struck me that we had been supposedly talking about music for twenty minutes, yet not once had the boys mentioned a song they liked or a guitarist who played well. Instead, the guys wanted to talk about drugs.

A great power lies in our talents, the power to influence others for good and for evil. What an awesome responsibility we have each day to use these talents well to build life and hope. (John)

Your story _____

• *Reflect on the gospel implications of a social issue, e.g., poverty, domestic violence, or land rights. Find out what the church teaches on this subject.*

• *How do these issues affect you personally?*

104

82) MATTHEW 22:15–21
Give therefore to the emperor the things that are the emperor's, and to God the things that are God's

Being Australian, being Christian

While getting ready for work one morning, I overheard a radio debate about a major basketball tournament that was being scheduled for the evening of Good Friday. Apparently the timing of the game had caused an outcry from the Christian churches. The radio interviewer was challenging a spokesperson for the Catholic Church on the issue. Although I heard only snatches of their conversation, it was enough to recognize a modern day re-enactment of Jesus' clever response to the Pharisees.

"What authority does a minority group have to dictate the schedule of a basketball game?" the interviewer was saying. "After all, millions of people love basketball, and everybody knows that the great Aussie sporting tradition is an essential part of a national holiday."

The Catholic spokesman quickly pointed out the hypocrisy of the question. The Good Friday holiday only existed because of a religious belief. If those who supported the scheduling of the game cared so much about the holiday, should they not also respect the convictions of the faith community responsible for its place in the calendar? Conversely, if the community's beliefs held no significance for the majority of Australians, would it not be more honest to cancel the holiday?

I smiled as I could almost hear Jesus say: "Give back to Australia what belongs to Australia—and to God what belongs to God."(Vincent)

Your story

- *Name the specific people to whom you are accountable (e.g. consider family, work, government, church).What tensions arise from demands placed on you?*
- *How do you handle conflicting responsibilities?*

83) MARK 11:1–10
Blessed is the one who comes in the name of the Lord

Suffering servants

On our visit to Czechoslovakia we stayed with Marie and Vic, a couple who had been leaders in an underground church during the days of Communist rule. Back in those days, their home would be transformed into a house church, with catechism being taught in one room, a prayer service going on in another, and a planning meeting in the attic. They were also involved in an illegal printing operation to produce Bibles. Consequently, they were a target of suspicion and their home was under constant surveillance by the authorities.

Marie recalls repeated incidents when, without a moment's notice, the police would descend on them and their modest little house would be ransacked. "They would search everything. Even the children's school bags. Then they would follow the children to school!" The children giggle at memories of dark-suited men trailing a five-year-old to kindergarten.

But life was far from funny in this Czech family's household. At one point Vic was jailed for several months. On another occasion their home was searched, inch by inch, over an entire weekend. The psychological strain was terrible. What sustained their commitment in the face of such danger? "We believed that God would be faithful to us," says Marie, simply. "We knew it was what God wanted us to do." (R and M)

Your story

- *In a relatively secure nation like the United States it is easy to turn our faith into comfortable Christianity. In light of this, what does it "cost" you to live by your convictions?*
- *What value does suffering have in your life?*

84) MARK 16:15–20
They went out and proclaimed the good news everywhere

Bibles and backpackers

"You're not reading that Christian stuff again, are you?"

The question came from the next bunk at the French youth hostel where my English friend and I had bedded down for the night. Jane and I were backpacking our way around the world. We had met somewhere in Greece and had been traveling together ever since.

In response to her question I read a passage from Luke's gospel in a loud, exaggerated voice while she groaned and put her head under the covers. It was our standard joke, our nightly ritual. I would read Scripture while Jane read a magazine, playfully teasing each other about our literary tastes. In Rome, however, things took an interesting twist.

Worn out from the day's activities I made a dismal attempt to open my Bible and instead felt myself dozing off.

"Aren't you going to read your Bible stuff tonight?" came Jane's voice through my sleepy fog.

"I thought you didn't like it."

"I don't, but I kinda miss it all the same."

"Read it yourself, then." I tossed the pocket Bible over to the next bunk where it hit its target.

"Ouch!"

That was the last I heard. At about two in the morning I awoke, growling at Jane for leaving the light on. I reached over to switch it off and there she was, wide awake, engrossed in the pages of that little Bible.

I couldn't believe it! All this time, I had considered Jane indifferent to religious belief. In fact, my friend had a hunger for the good news!

Your story _____

• *What are some of simple, everyday ways you have seen people spread good news, bad news, and the "good news" message of Jesus Christ?*

• *How comfortable are you in reading Scripture? Where does this practice fit in your prayer life, if at all?*

85) MATTHEW 15:21–28
Great is your faith! Let it be done for you as you wish

Under pressure

Today I witnessed the gospel at work while riding on a New York City bus. It was during rush hour traffic, when there was that "pressure cooker" feeling about the whole city. A passenger boarded who clearly had a mental disability as he struggled to communicate with the bus driver.

"I'm sorry, sir, I'm having difficulty understanding. What ticket do you require?"

The passenger continued to speak and gesture, but he wasn't getting through.

Helpfully, the driver held open his folder of tickets. "Can you point to the ticket you need, sir?"

The dialogue struggled along until the bus driver figured out that the man required a certain kind of weekly pass.

"Sir, we don't sell those on this bus. You have to purchase it at another place. But don't worry—how about you take a seat now and you can pick up that pass another time?" The man gratefully sat down and the journey continued.

As I got off the bus, I made a point of speaking to the driver: "You know, you were very kind and respectful toward that man," I said. It was true. He could easily have boiled over with impatience and ordered him off. But in front of a busful of passengers and under the pressure of his schedule he displayed patience and empathy. (Jill)

Your story _____

- *Describe a scene where gospel values overcame what could have been a prejudiced response.*
- *In what ways have you overcome prejudice in your own life?*
- *This week, notice someone who might be considered on the fringes of society. Make an effort to include them in a conversation or activity.*

86) LUKE 9:51–62
Go and proclaim the kingdom of God

Buried treasure

My husband and I were invited to join a prayer group. It was all pretty new to us, but we went along and discovered we enjoyed meeting each week with these people. Still, it wasn't the kind of activity I broadcasted. At work, for instance, I talked freely about my weekly tennis lessons and the TV programs I watched, but I never mentioned our prayer group.

One evening, I went to a town meeting. There, two of my husband's friends recognized me and came over for a chat.

"Hey, aren't you supposed to be at your counseling group tonight?" asked one.

"What?" I asked, totally confused by his question.

"You know, the prayer counseling thing that you go to every week," said the other.

My face started to turn crimson as I realized the strange reference was to our prayer group. My husband must have said something to these guys! I came clean.

"Oh, you mean our prayer group. No, it's nothing to do with counseling. It's a…uh…it's a group of people who get together and chat about their week and pray a bit…"

As they continued to question me I realized these guys were completely sincere. With no religious background they were having difficulty understanding exactly what the group was, but they knew it was something to do with Christianity and they were genuinely intrigued.

I learned a lesson that night. There are people out there who are sincerely open to hearing about Jesus—but they've never had the opportunity. And I learned that, if I stopped being so defensive about my faith, I just might be able to offer them something. (Cathy)

Your story

• *Reflect on your faith as a gift to be shared and "invested": have you used this gift well? How have you "buried" it?*
• *What risks are involved in sharing your faith?*

109

87) MARK 1:14–20
Follow me and I will make you fish for people

No stopping us now

Our nineteen-year-old daughter had mentioned a few times that she would like to go to Africa to work as a missionary. At first I thought it was just a whim. But when my husband and I realized that her desire was genuine, we decided to encourage her. We began to share our experience of what it meant to put God first in our lives. We explained to her that there would be moments of darkness, but also tremendous joys.

One evening she came home and I could see she had been crying. I asked her if she wanted to share what was troubling her. She immediately expressed what was in her heart: "Now I know what it is to leave everything like it says in the gospel. It really means everything doesn't it, Mom? My stereo, my CDs and tapes, and not having the car when I need it. It means leaving you, Dad, and the rest of the kids." Her understanding of this touched me.

A few nights later she came into our bedroom and sat on the end of the bed, asking questions about going away. At first the questions were quite superficial, but after a while she said, "Dad, could it happen that I might be killed or die in Africa?" He said, "Yes, you could, but we can't let that stop us, otherwise we would never do anything for God." This answer may have come as a shock to her but she seemed happy and went off to bed.

The day came for her to leave. There were, of course, a few tears, but all had been said on both sides during the previous weeks and months. It was up to God to take care of her from now on. (M.D.) (Courtesy, *The World of Families*, Focolare Movement, 1994)

Your story

- *What have you "left behind" in order to be a follower of Jesus Christ?*
- *How have you encouraged someone to be faithful to God's call?*

JOHN 14:15–21
In a little while the world will no longer see me, but you will see me; because I live, you also will live

Remain in my love

My Uncle Mark—always the picture of health and fitness—died suddenly of heart failure. It was a great shock for the whole family. Eighteen months later, crazy things remind me of him: like pancakes (which he loved to make on Sunday mornings); like anything to do with football (Mark was a sports fanatic); like my Reebok sneakers that I bought just before I went on vacation with his family. I also remember how he and my aunt would sit around the table with me after dinner and offer suggestions on how I could use my nursing degree. Uncle Mark was always so supportive, and encouraged me to be the best I could be, whether it was in my health, my work, or my relationships with other people.

I remember the way he would say grace before meals with a gentle, good-humored flamboyance. He was a man of great faith with a knack of making religion seem joyous and fun, while still a presenting a challenge.

I feel a real emptiness now that he has gone. And yet, I also feel his presence with me in so many ways. Ironically, so many memories have been built through tiny, trivial events, the so-called "wasted" time like holidays and just family "hanging around" together. I guess this time is never trivial or wasted, but a precious way in which families build memories and pass on their values.

Six months after the death of his father, one of Mark's sons made this comment: "Although Dad's no longer here in a physical way, our relationship continues. To me it feels like it is still growing. I'm changing, even as Dad's life has most certainly been changed. It's a matter of exploring our relationship in a whole new way." (Tina)

Your story

- *How does your family build memories of love?*
- *What difference does your faith make to your capacity to love and be loved?*
- *Name those tiny habits which are essential to building a loving home: e.g., praise, affection, time together, noticing each other's gifts, prayer.*

12

Stories
of Joy

89) JOHN 9:1–41
He was born blind so that God's works might be revealed in him

Live life to the full

When I first arrived in Manila for a six-month stay, I was overwhelmed by the sheer filth, the smog, the broken walkways, the unfinished buildings that dotted the skyline, the chaotic traffic.

Yet, in the midst of this seeming chaos, there was something more. It became most obvious when we visited the leprosarium at Tala and heard them say: "Thanks for visiting us. Thank you!" In central Manila, the street children clung to us for recognition and affection, and in the local jail we heard political prisoners tell their tale of torture and sing of freedom. At the Payatas dumpsites—a scene of human misery and injustice—we gratefully accepted the people's offer of a drink and a biscuit which they could not afford to give, but did so anyway.

In all this, I began to sense a joy of living. I experienced a fun-loving, dancing, singing, laughing people who lived in the midst of real deprivation. They are destitute. They are insecure. They are injustly treated. Yet they have a true sense of life.

The Payatas are at the extreme end of the spectrum of poverty and injustice. But to me they represent the totality of the Filipino people. When they are sad, they show it. When they are unjustly treated, they are not downhearted. When they celebrate, all the world celebrates with them.

So now, as I am about to leave the Philippines, I go away with a very different attitude. I now see that our middle-class way of life—clean and well provided for—may be somewhat sterile, lacking life. I hope I can learn to cherish my life, show gratitude for a helping hand, sing of my freedom, celebrate my joys, and value my family and friends like the people I have met here. (Noel)

Your story _____

- *How does my life-style cushion me from mixing with those who are seemingly poor, sinners, and the outcasts of society?*
- *Would you describe yourself as a joyful person? Why or why not? What are the characteristics of joy?*

90)

Luke 7:1–10

Lord, do not trouble yourself, for I am not worthy to have you come under my roof

Dad's house

Selling Dad's house was one of the saddest things I have ever had to do. It really brought home to me the reality of his death. Dad had always been a figure of life and energy, a sprightly and humorous man even in his later years. Our family had spent many happy hours together in his big family home enjoying good food and good company. We also were treated to good music, as Dad reveled in entertaining us with his musical prowess. But now he was gone. And sadly, this house of treasured memories had to go as well.

At first I was disappointed with the way the auction went. The house didn't sell for anywhere near the price we had hoped for. "Oh well," I thought. "That's the way things go." Some weeks later, however, I had the opportunity to meet the new owners. What a delightful surprise! Dad would have loved these new occupants. Not only were they lovely people, but they had a good number of children and grandchildren and a wonderful sense of family. We had assumed that a new owner would pull down the little cottage at the back of the house. But in fact these people planned to keep it just as it was so that their extended family could come to stay—just as we had when Dad was alive!

And do you know what else? The new owners are a family full of musicians! The mother teaches at a conservatory and all the children play at least one instrument. Looking back at my reaction after the auction, I think: who cares about the money? If it means Dad's home continues to be filled with love, life, and music then it was the perfect sale. (Julie)

Your story

- *Describe one of the most life-giving people you know.*
- *Who has given you life (physically, spiritually, emotionally)? Have you ever thanked them?*
- *Is there a part of you that feels "dead"? What is one life-giving step you can take to bring this part to life? How can your faith help in the process?*

91) LUKE 9:28–36
And while he was praying, the appearance of his face changed, and his clothes became dazzling white

A different side to Dorothy

You probably would not recognize me if you saw me on the street. After all, I look like an ordinary person—except when I am at work. Then, to millions of children who are fans of the well-known children's rock band, "The Wiggles," I am "Dorothy the Dinosaur," a lovable six-foot character in a green dinosaur suit!

One afternoon, the Wiggles had a gig at a children's hospital. Whenever we do a regular show for children, Dorothy comes down and greets all the kids after the performance. This is a real "Santa Claus" experience, as all the children come rushing forward and climb all over you: it makes me feel like Christmas! Well, on this particular day everything went as planned. I opened my big dinosaur arms, and there was this swarm of little kids cuddling into me, wide-eyed with wonder, squealing with delight.

But something was different, too. These little children wore caps to cover the bald spots from their radiation treatment. Some had intravenous drips attached to their arms. Others had to be carried, so weak were their cancer-ravaged little bodies. Inside that crazy dinosaur suit, my heart was melting at the incongruity of the scene; that out of such a "silly" theatrical moment, God's love could suddenly become so tangible; that in the midst of this wave of human suffering and brokenness, I could be engulfed by such wonder and joy. This time, it wasn't a Santa Claus feeling that I had; it was a Christ-experience, a rare and privileged moment of being touched by pure, childlike love. I tell you, these little ones in hospital know something about life which we "well and able" adults can so easily miss. (JF)

Your story

- *What can children teach us about love, hope, faith, God?*
- *Describe a moment when you turned to God with a worry, a burden, a cry for help. What came about as a result of this?*
- *What barriers do you sometimes set up between yourself and God?*

The kingdom is here!

One weekend recently I attended a retreat. There I fell in love all over again, with God and with my husband, Matt. But unfortunately, Matt wasn't on the retreat. He was fifty miles away back home, preparing to drive north on a business trip.

On the second day of the retreat I had such an intense and overpowering feeling of love for Matt that I called him up and said: "I've just got to see you, even if it's just a glimpse!" To my delight, Matt was feeling the same way. He was, however, just about to set out on his trip and there was no time for us to meet. The route he was going to take ran nearby the retreat house, so we were able to arrange a rather crazy rendezvous. We decided that I would stand on the bridge over the nearby freeway between 4:45 and 5:45 in the afternoon, wearing bright clothes, while Matt was to come driving down flicking his headlights on and off.

When the time came, I waited on the bridge as planned, feeling more like an excited teenager than a woman married for twenty-five years. Ah! There was Matt, the car headlights flashing like crazy. I felt a great thrill as I waved and waved to the man of my life—God's greatest gift to me. I stood waving into the distance for a long time until his car was just a speck on the horizon.

Perhaps you need to know Matt and I (and our particular brand of humor) to appreciate this story, but let me tell you, the freeway incident was one of the highlights of my retreat. (Jacinta)

Your story _____

• *Jacinta describes Matt as "God's greatest gift to me." Who is one of God's greatest gifts to you?*
• *Describe a time you were filled with an overpowering sense of love and an urgency to do something about it. What did you do?*
• *How is God "near" to you in the people and events of your life?*

93) LUKE 1:26–38
The child to be born will be holy; he will be called Son of God

Sharing the spirit of Christmas

Coming home from work on the train one Christmas Eve, I felt overcome by a sense of—what shall I call it—reverence? The realization of Christ's birth really struck home and in response I began to softly sing Christmas carols to myself. (I am a music teacher, and so singing is second nature to me.) While at first I felt rather self-conscious among the rush-hour crowd on the train, an awareness of the holiness of this evening continued to well within me, making any resistance seem futile. And so, as the train whizzed along, I continued my caroling: *Silent Night, Away in the Manger, O Come All Ye Faithful*....

After a while I became aware of a background hum. My goodness— people were singing along! With new confidence I began to sing a little louder and, as I did so, the accompanying voices rose too. Then I noticed something else. As passengers reached their destination they were deliberately walking down to my end of the carriage to nod "thanks" as they alighted from the train. One woman even stopped to say that she had tried all day to no avail to get her office staff into the festive spirit. So she was especially grateful for the chance to celebrate Christmas on the way home from work.

Given the usual body language that prevails on public transportation ("Don't invade my space"), the whole train ride was a rather graced event. It was a Christmas Eve I won't easily forget! (Lee)

Your story

- *What does Christmas mean to you? How do you share the Christmas spirit with other people?*
- *What does it mean to be a "good news" person?*
- *Talk about simple ways we can use our gifts and talents to bring life and joy to others.*

118

94) JOHN 20:1–9
They have taken the Lord out of the tomb

Easter image

Have you noticed how the simplest things can bring joy? Like compost. Our family compost bin has brought many laughs to our conversations as my father proudly nurtures the warm, fuming organic mass in the corner of his backyard. Food scraps are treated with reverence and ceremoniously fed into the magic bin. The result is a continuous supply of pumpkins, tomatoes and watermelon plants sprouting in unexpected places in the backyard. You see, wherever the compost is spread, the seeds hidden in the mulch find a niche in the soil and start to grow.

Grace at work is a bit like that, don't you think? God can use even the discarded and wasted parts of our lives to bring forth new shoots of life and love. (Kristina)

Easter at the airport

I will always remember the day Sam's family arrived from Vietnam. Our friend Sam had escaped to Australia four years earlier after spending six years in prison under Communist rule.

As he established a new life in Australia he struggled with the language, worked long hours in an unfulfilling job, and patiently waded through government bureaucracy as he persisted in his quest to be reunited with his family. During those years, Sam never lost heart. He placed his entire life and that of his family in the hands of God. When we eventually had the privilege of welcoming his family on Australian soil at Sydney airport in 1987, it was like a dream come true. (Claire)

Your story

• *How has a painful experience led to a new experience of joy? How has a new door opened as a result of another closing?*
• *What does Easter mean to you?*
• *How can we live as "Easter people" all year long?*

The millionaire

He came to the doctor's office, where I worked as a receptionist, for his annual check-up. He was a lovely Italian man of about seventy, always so positive and a joy to have in the waiting room because he lifted everyone's spirits. He had migrated to the States about forty years ago with nothing but the clothes he wore and the equivalent of $5.00 in his pocket. The light of his life was his family—his wife Claudia and ten children. I gradually came to know most of them as they took turns accompanying their father on his annual visits. They were an impressive family in the way they cared for each other.

On this day, he was very excited. He had recently revisited Italy and looked up his old school friends. Apparently, they were all doctors and lawyers who wore expensive suits. The man went into considerable detail telling me about his successful classmates. As for himself, he explained apologetically, he was just a laborer. He showed me his hands, rough and gnarled as if to prove his point. He had worked so hard all his life, but wealth and status were not his lot.

"But you have a beautiful wife and ten children!" I exclaimed. "Why, you are a millionaire! Money has only finite value. A loving family is priceless."

His reaction took me by surprise. His chest puffed out with pride, while his eyes lit up and glistened with tears. It occurred to me that this man had never before been praised for his greatest treasure. (Renee)

Your story

• *Describe someone you know who is very "rich"; not materially but in terms of human qualities and relationships.*
• *To get rich materially we usually have to work very hard, save, and invest wisely. How do we get rich in non-material ways? What do we have to work hard at?*
• *What are some of the true riches of your own life?*

96)
JOHN 2:1–12
You have kept the good wine until now

An Easter street

Ten neighbors in our street were all turning fifty, so they decided to throw a baby boomers party. What a night! Half the street was closed to cars, a tarpaulin was erected and decorated, local shops were asked to provide meat for the barbeque, and everyone pitched in with salads, drinks, and a homespun disco. What a delight to see neighbors of all ages partying together. The scene of little tots, teenagers, parents, and grandparents all dancing the macarena was a sight to behold!

Well, the party was such a winner that this casual little social committee of talented entrepreneurs decided their next project would be a garage sale involving all the families on the entire street. That project, too, was a success in building relationships and good humor. It just goes to show the impact a few well-motivated neighbors can have. Even an ordinary suburban street can elicit a host of gifts and talents and generate so much life and joy. (Tina)

Queen Emily

Emily is the youngest of our seven children. At a family meal on the eve of her First Communion Day, all her big brothers and sisters dressed up in formal attire—suits, bow ties, evening dresses, the works—and made it a very special occasion in her honor. Pretty amazing given that the standard dress for a significant portion of our household is jeans and sneakers! We had a lot of laughs and Emily felt like a queen.

The body of Christ we received the next day was all the more significant because of the presence of Christ we had celebrated in one another the night before. (M and MJ)

Your story _____

- *Reflect on a "good news" story which happened in your own life.*
- *What are some of the simple ways you give and receive life?*

121

Backpacker

In our pharmacy today I served an eighty-four-year-old lady who is backpacking her way around Australia. She stays in youth hostels en route and yes, she had the backpack and all the appropriate gear. She told me that she spends a good part of her year traveling like this. "I get rather lonely at home," she explained. "Everyone in my apartment complex keeps to themselves. But the young people I meet in the youth hostels are so friendly and open and love to chat." (Jackie)

A face in the crowd

At the park I recognized a young woman in a wheelchair. We had met five years earlier at a special school for the deaf and blind where she was a fifteen-year-old resident, and I was employed as a pastoral worker.

As I approached her I noticed that her health had rapidly deteriorated—not just her sight and hearing but her muscle movements as well. I made myself known to her by pressing sign language into the palm of her hand. To my delight, she remembered me. Her next question took me aback: "How did you recognize me? Was it my face or my wheelchair?" (WD)

Your Story _____

    • *How do you live out your baptismal call to bring the Word of God to the world?*
    • *Do you find it difficult to live out God's call in our increasingly materialistic and secular society? How do you counter these cultural influences?*

98) MATTHEW 6:21–27

For where your treasure is, there your heart will be also

Where Madonna lost the plot

While watching a TV program about the pop idol Madonna, I could not help but be impressed by her talent, drive, and self-assurance. Toward the end of the show, she summed up her life with this emphatic statement: I am my own work of art.

As if to challenge the direction of my admiration, at Mass the following day a line from Scripture leapt out at me. It was from Paul's letter to the Ephesians, and it said simply: "For we are what he has made us, created in Christ Jesus for good works, which God prepared beforehand to be our way of life" (2:10).

I have since pondered this contrast many times. How subtly we can turn our God-given gifts into self-made achievements, forgetting the giver and creating our own gods. (Anna)

Living the questions

A seventeen-year-old boy committed suicide just before his final exams. His mother had lost her husband four years before and was just recovering from that grief when her son died.

This woman is involved in the local church, a faithful parishioner with enormous unresolved questions, forever trying to understand "Why?" Just to see her at church is an inspiration to me. She has every reason to give up—but she has not. (Therese)

Your Story

- *Where does your treasure lie? How do you use it? Do you believe this comes from your own doing or can you see the hand of God in your life?*
- *Are there any particular Scripture passages that give you courage in the face of death? hope in light of suffering? strength in times of adversity? Over the next few weeks, read through your Bible and try to find words or phrases that can help in your spiritual growth.*

99) MARK 10:2–16

Let the little children come to me; do not stop them; for it is to such as these that the kingdom of God belongs

Proclamation!

My four-year-old niece had been watching a video about the life of Jesus Christ. Consequently, at our next family gathering she was running around declaring at the top of her lungs, "Jesus died on the cross to save us...poor Jesus...and Mary was very sad. But then he came alive again!" Little actress that she is, her voice and facial expressions reeked with pathos. With about a dozen adults standing around, I saw people genuinely being touched by the innocence of a little child unabashedly telling the gospel story. (TP)

Simple joys

At her father's funeral, twelve-year-old Emily placed a picture of an ice cream cone on the coffin. She described it as "a symbol of Dad's simplicity." Her father, while moving easily in the circles of high-powered professionals, had never lost sight of life's simple joys and pleasures, like sharing an ice cream with his youngest daughter. Says Emily: "Whenever we were out and about Dad would often say to me, 'Emily, I think it's time for an ice cream cone!'"

Your Story _____

- *Describe a time when you were healed by faith. Was there a turning point in the process? What happened?*
- *What are some of the simple joys which you enjoy with family and friends?*
- *How are you childlike in your faith and in your deeds?*

100) JOHN 17:1–11
I glorified you on earth by finishing the work that you gave me to do

The journey we made together

Seven years ago, Peter and Chele, a married couple in their late thirties, prepared for the darkest moment of their lives: separation through death. At great cost they learned what many of us have yet to learn: in the end love is all we have and all that matters.

Chele was diagnosed with inoperable cancer in 1988. For the next 18 months, the two of us journeyed together through chemotherapy, radiation therapy, and visits to hospitals and specialists. By October 1989, she could no longer walk. The cancer had eaten through her spine. There were blood transfusions, spasms, tears, and pain. We made the decision that we would care for her at home, and Chele's parents came to live with us and be of help.

Throughout Chele's illness there was one thing and only one thing that kept us going: love for each other. This love was shared through the pain of our trials and the joy of what we meant to each other.

A few days before Chele's death we held a family birthday party at our home. One can only imagine the sadness of that day. Yet it was Chele who started singing "Happy Birthday," as loud as her weakened voice would allow. Her goodness again had gone out to us all.

Later that night Chele asked me the most difficult question I will ever be asked: "Is there anything anyone can do for me?" I had to reply in truth: "No, dear." Chele trusted me to be completely honest with her. Our love had given us that bond of truth.

After she died, many people came to Chele's funeral at St Patrick's Church, where we had been married just six years earlier. People wrote to me about the way Chele had affected them with her love of life. She endured more than most people are ever called to endure. (Peter)

Your story

- *Our love stories are precious because they reveal the face of God in our lives. What is your own unique love story?*

Index of Gospel passages

Reading .... Page

Matthew

1:18–24	71
2:1–12	94
5:1–12	68
5:13–16	5
5:16–37	76
6:21–27	123
6:24–34	57
9:9–13	7
9:36—10:8	65
10:26–33	9
10:37–42	91
11:2–11	117
11:25–30	28
13:1–23	39
13:31–35	4
13:44–52	74
14:22–36	34
15:21–28	108
16:13–23	120
16:21–27	6
18:15–20	25
18:21–35	26
20:1–16	35
21:33–43	104
22:15–21	105
23:1–12	88
24:37–44	38
25:1–13	19
25:14–30	97
25:31–46	18
26:14—27:66	16
28:1–10	30
28:16–20	122

Reading .... Page

Mark

1:12–15	40
1:14–20	110
1:29–39	95
4:35–44	100
6:1–6	66
6:7–13	10
6:30–34	15
7:1–8, 14–15, 21–23	45
7:31–37	89
8:27–35	47
9:30–37	77
10:2–16	124
10:35–45	48
11:1–10	106
12:28–34	8
12:38–44	78
14:12–16, 22–26	41
14:1—15:47	14
16:15–20	107

Luke

1:1–4	11
1:26–38	118
2:22–40	70
4:14–21	67
6:27–38	24
7:1–10	115
7:36—8:3	80
9:11–17	81
9:28–36	116
9:51–62	109
10:1–12,17–20	79
10:25–37	51
10:38–42	46

Reading .... Page

11:1–13	59
12:13–21	84
13:1–9	90
14:1, 7–14	75
16:1–13	69
16:19–31	50
17:11–19	21
18:1–8	96
18:9–14	29
20:27–38	54
22:14—23:56	87
23:35–46	99
24:13–35	17

John

1:1–18	61
2:1–12	121
3:14–21	44
3:16–18	56
4:5–42	37
6:41–51	58
6:51–58	101
8:1–11	49
9:1–41	114
10:11–18	86
11:1–45	60
14:1–12	64
14:15–21	111
15:1–8	98
15:9–17	27
16:12–15	55
17:1–11	125
18:1—19:42	20
18:33–37	85
20:1–9	119
20:19–31	31
21:1–19	36

Of Related Interest

A World of Stories for Preachers and Teachers*

*and all who love stories that move and challenge

Rev. William J. Bausch

These newest tales (350!) from Fr. Bausch are not just a plateful of "literary Twinkies" but an immense and varied menu with rich meals, wholesome lunches, snacks, and even "playful fare." They range in length from a paragraph to several pages. This book should be in the hands of every preacher, storyteller, teacher, and reader—indeed, every person seeking to impart or gain wisdom.

ISBN: 0-89622-919-X
544 pp, $29.95

Everyday Epiphanies

Seeing the Sacred in Every Thing

Melannie Svoboda, SND

Offers 175 short stories with topics ranging from the ordinary to the uncommon occasions that we all look forward to and relish. A comprehensive index cross references topics and themes to stories. Scripture passages scattered throughout offer insights into the ways that Jesus used the occurrences of everyday living to reveal both God and grace.

ISBN: 0-89622-730-8
200 pp, $9.95

Stories for all Seasons

For Every Sunday, Every Year, Every Preacher, Every Teacher

Gerard Fuller, OMI

Offers a collection of stories related to all the Sunday Gospel readings for the three-year cycle. A great resource for priests, catechists, teachers—anyone who wants to use the power of story to make the Sunday gospel come alive.

ISBN: 0-89622-643-3
160 pp, $12.95

Coincidences

Touched by a Miracle

Antoinette Bosco

Here the author has collected an impressive kaleidoscope of stories about real people from all walks of life who experienced what might be called a "remarkable coincidence" in their lives. Are the patterns of their life stories really random? Or is there an underlying design common to all, a design that reveals the hand and the presence of Someone who cares? This book will appeal to all who seek inspiration, who need a boost in their faith in God and in people, or who teach through story.

ISBN: 0-89622-749-9
208 pp, $12.95

Available at religious bookstores or from:

XXIII **TWENTY-THIRD PUBLICATIONS**
P.O. Box 180 • Mystic, CT 06355 • 1-800-321-0411